A Guide to
Medieval English Tithe Barns

BY JAMES W. GRISWOLD

To Anna Melotti — With hope that as a Britam and as an architect you will have a double pleasure.

Jim Griswold

PETER E. RANDALL PUBLISHER
PORTSMOUTH, NEW HAMPSHIRE
1999

In the northern stretches of the Vale of the Whitehorse, some two miles southwest of the town of Faringdon in Berkshire, there rises the finest medieval barn in England, the barn of the Abbey Grange of Great Coxwell. The great lines of its simple mass, the intersecting bodies of its two large transeptal porches, the steep ascent of its gables, and the noble silhouette of its vast roof are unsurpassed by any structure of like design. Moreover, in the interior, supporting the roof, this barn displays one of the most magnificent frames of medieval timber ever known in a building of this construction type. In no other surviving structure of this kind are the basic architectural capabilities of wood so forcibly and convincingly expressed: its ability to carry huge compressive loads on slender and remarkably high uprights, and its incredible tensile strength, enabling it to bridge intervals of extraordinary width and depth, to penetrate space, to embrace it, and thus to retain within a structure internally divided into a multitude of separate cells an overpowering sense of spatial wholeness.

William Morris, who was within walking distance of the barn of Great Coxwell while living at Kelmscott House, loved this building so passionately that he proclaimed it to be "the finest piece of architecture in England."

—From *The Barns of the Abbey of Beaulieu at its Granges of Great Coxwell and Beaulieu St. Leonards,* Walter Horn and Ernest Born, 1965.

Great Coxwell, Berkshire, exterior from the southwest, built about 1230. (Print used with permission, from Horn and Born, *The Barns of the Abbey of Beaulieu,* 1965.

To my wife of 65 years who was with me on all our trips, who kept the maps folded to the right pages, who sometimes navigated with exciting results, who learned to spot a barn before I could, who could charm any stranger, who could easily adjust to any level of accomodations, and who is just plain fun.

Copyright © 1999 by James W. Griswold.
Printed in the United States of America

Design; Tom Allen, Pear Graphics

Peter E. Randall Publisher
Box 4726
Portsmouth, New Hampshire 03802-4726

Distributed by University Press of New England
Hanover and London

Library of Congress Cataloging-in-Publication Data
Griswold, James W., 1909

A guide to medieval English tithe barns / by James W. Griswold.
    p. c m .
Includes bibliographical references.
ISBN 0-914339-73-7
    1. Tithe barns—England. 2. Architecture, Medieval—England.
I. Title.
NA8230.G75 1999
728'.922'09420902—dc2l

99-18370
CIP

Special thanks are due to my personal editor, Adrien J. Kant, who converted the original manuscript into a book. Her questions, corrections, and suggestions helped make the project understandable, logical, and interesting.

Bonnie Boone Day Griswold,
the most important helper on this project.
(Please see Dedication)

Our four daughters, Susan, Jane, Betsy, and Lucinda, all of whom helped, but especially Susan, who insisted I do this project and then gave me encouragement, help, and guidance with all its details as well as many hours of her time.

Sons-in-law Tom Blandy, who did many of the fine descriptive drawings, and Norman Vershay, who helped me with my photography techniques.

Utterly essential was the help given by our English friends, Mr. and Mrs. Roy McLeod and Mr. and Mrs. David Patterson, who provided annual housing in the Stratford area, contacts, and advice when necessary.

Doris Troy, the publisher's editor, whose standards are higher than any college English professor.

Walter Horn and Ernest Born, whose beautiful book on the Great Coxwell barn published in 1963 was an inspiration.

FWB and Mary Charles, who entertained us in their home, and Mr. Charles, who took us to the Bredon barn during his supervision of the reconstruction after the fire of 1980.

Cecil Hewett, for his scholarly book on English historic carpentry.

Graham Hughes for his book on *Barns of Rural Britain*.

Nikon Cameras and Eastman Kodak Company for their excellent products. Ben's Photo Shop in Exeter, New Hampshire, for help and advice. All photographs were taken by the author unless otherwise indicated.

And finally, for his vision and experience, the publisher, Peter Randall, who is an expert.

CONTENTS

An Overview

WELCOME!

We hope you find this book both enjoyable and instructive.

By the time you have turned to this page, you have probably looked at the photograph on the cover, and you have leafed through the pages to check out the interior pictures to get the feel of the book. We hope by now it has passed your inspection, and you have bought the book.

Or maybe someone has given it to you thinking you would find it interesting, and you are skeptical. Based on the fun we have had with the subject, we hope you will give the book some of your time. We think you will find it very worthwhile.

(Opposite)
Cressing Temple, Essex, the Barley barn, interior, circa 1130-1200.

Buckland Abbey, Devon, interior, 150 by 32 and 60 feet high, circa 1300.

How We Learned About Tithe Barns

Our interest in Tithe Barns started when we were on our first trip to England. We had with us our oldest daughter, who had majored in architectural history, and her husband, who is an architect. We saw the usual wonderful structures that England has in great quantity, quality, and variety. Then one morning our daughter and her husband told us we were going to see something quite different.

They took us to the Great Coxwell Tithe Barn located about twenty miles southwest of Oxford. As a boy, in the 1920s, when I visited my grandfather's farm in Indiana, I had become familiar with large barns and had played in the hay, sliding from a position close to the top of the roof down to the wooden floor where the wagons came in to unload. But Great Coxwell, with intricate timbers holding up the roof, was much bigger, more open, grander, higher and, of course, many times older.

Great Coxwell, Berkshire, 152 by 43 and 48 feet high, circa 1230.

There is a very special feeling that comes to you as you enter a Tithe Barn. It is parallel to, but in contrast to, the feeling you get when you enter a great cathedral. In the cathedral, there is a sense of magnitude as you come to the center aisle just inside the western facade and see the great columns of the nave recede successively toward the choir. But the cathedral by its very nature is full of distractions: tombs, memorials, decorations, flags and, yes, even beautiful flowers. Further, the great height of the elaborate ceiling that you see is not the true roof of the building, but rather an interior envelope separating you from the real roof.

In direct contrast, when you enter a Tithe Barn, you see everything. There are no distractions. The function of every part of the building is directly related to its function as a whole. The roof you see is the structure that protects the interior contents of the barn from rain, snow and wind. The tremendous weight of the roof is clearly directed through the oak timbers to the upright columns within the stone walls and down to the floor. The simple naked skeleton of the barn is beautiful.

(Left) Interior roof detail of barn at Coggeshall.

Coggeshall, Essex, interior of restored barn, possibly the oldest barn in England, circa 1140.

Since that first visit to the Great Coxwell barn, we have made many trips to England, searched out what printed information we could find on English barns and early English carpentry, and visited—and revisited—at least half the barns listed in this book. We traveled to many sites where our early information listed a barn, only to discover that it had burned down or otherwise been destroyed. Because of this, we learned not only about barns but also about English history. It has been enlightening and fun.

If you think you might like to:

· get off the thruways
· see the real English countryside
· visit with people in their homes or at their work
· have a pub lunch in a small town
· enjoy a roadside English garden
· drive down a road only wide enough for one car, and have to back into a layby
· see a rainbow or a sunset across newly harvested fields
· be delayed by a herd of cows on the road being driven by a farmer and his dog from one field to another
· or even just get lost,

then searching for early English barns is highly recommended.

This book has been prepared by Americans. Occasionally you will find references and comparisons to American agriculture. Also, because of the newness of our country, you will find a special appreciation for the antiquity of these Tithe Barns. We find sometimes that the English residents become hardened by being surrounded by great, old structures and miss the thrill that can come to an American visitor when viewing a farm building that is seven hundred years old and still in use.

Another hint to the American reader: The English word "corn" should be translated by the American as wheat, barley or rye, grown primarily for human consumption. It does not refer to our wonderful field corn that is grown mainly for animal feed. England's climate generally does not grow good field corn, and it has been grown in the southern part of the island only recently. It was not a food source in the time of the Tithe Barn.

What Is a Tithe Barn?

In this book, we concentrate only on barns built after 1066, when William I came across from Normandy, and before 1555, when Henry VIII seized the monasteries and set up the Church of England. There is only one known remnant of a barn built in the Saxon period before 1066.[1] There were many barns built after 1555, but they are less interesting structurally and so are not included here.

Technically, a Tithe Barn was a structure built by a monastery or the bishop of a diocese to store the tithe share (one tenth) of the produce of the land. The tithe was collected as a tax from the parishioners to support the work of the church or monastery. Agriculture was the primary source of wealth, and the Tithe Barn served as the bank for the religious institution. There was very little money in circulation, as most obligations were paid with produce.

The church at this time was the major social force and power in society, much more important than any royal institution. The church took care of the religious needs of nearly everyone. It was also the only educational and learning center for all of Europe. It educated its own clerics and also the children of the royal and noble families. The church was the only organization to care for the poor and the sick, which it did as best it could. The church kept property records, records of baptism, marriage, and burial, and ran a court of justice, which decided most of the disputes among the people and served them well. For travelers, the church was a place for food and rest at the end of the day. And because the language of the church all over Europe was Latin, a traveler who knew Latin could easily move from one country to another.

The Tithe Barn was very important for the operation of this religious society. Records indicate that upon the founding of a monastery, the barn was the first building to be constructed, so that the group could collect enough resources to build the church. This means that in some locations, the barn is older than the adjoining church. The Tithe Barns, as the banks for the church, evidently provided the necessary support.

During the time to which this book refers, England saw a greater building boom, with more construction—much of which was of churches and castles—than at any previous time in its history. Then, after 1500, general construction was not so active until the boom of post World War II. Between 1100 and 1500, England built twenty-six major cathedrals and thousands of parish churches. It is estimated that more than two thousand barns were built at this time, some even larger than any barns now standing.

Not all barns built during this period were strictly for storing tithes. Owners of large amounts of land had barns for their own use, which did not belong to the church. Such barns look like many other large barns of this period; a search of the early records to determine original ownership can sometimes be very difficult. So, for our purposes, all large barns that were built during this time we call Tithe Barns. This may irritate the more careful historical scholars, but we have found some barns that served both masters. Certain barns that may not have been built to store tithes are included here because they are historically important. Furthermore,

Door of barn at Buckland Abbey, Devon. Careful inspection of the stone trim at the base of the arch will reveal a vertical slot where a board could be inserted to keep the threshed grain inside the barn on the threshing floor and at the same time allow the chaff to blow over and out.

the British public tend to use the word "tithe" rather loosely to designate any very old barn, sometimes only to enhance its romance upon conversion into a restaurant or dwelling.

What Is a Tithe Barn Used For?

The barns of this period do seem not to have been used for the protection of animals, as American barns are. This is because the English winters are not as severe, and their animals are bred for their rugged endurance. Also, the barns were not needed for the storage of winter animal feed as they are in America, where winter grazing is not possible.

These structures are so large, however, because in addition to serving as a storehouse for farm products, the Tithe Barn also served as a workspace after harvest. In late summer and fall, grain was cut in the fields and brought to the barn to ripen, thus reducing the loss of the precious crop in the field. It was stored in loose mows and well ventilated, because if it was packed tight, there was a danger of spontaneous combustion.

The big doors on opposite sides of the barn were opened and a baffle board was inserted at the threshold (please note the word) to restrain the grain, while letting the wind blow the chaff outside when the sheaves were beaten on the stone floor with a flail. A flail is an ancient farm tool consisting of a solid wood stick about five feet long to which is loosely attached by a leather thong a lighter wooden stick about three feet in length. The operator skillfully swung the heavy stick

Threshing depicted by using a flail. This method of separating the grain from the straw is shown accurately, but the early-nineteenth-century clothing of the men may show how little change had taken place in this method of threshing for the preceding five hundred years. Picture hangs in the barn-restaurant of the National Trust property Baddesley Clinton in Warwickshire.

Bredon barn, Worcestershire, acrial view from the south-east. Note outside stairway leading to a small room with fireplace and chimney for the resident clerk who could supervise building and contents. (Drawing used with permission from *The Great Barn at Bredon*, by F.W.B. Charles.)

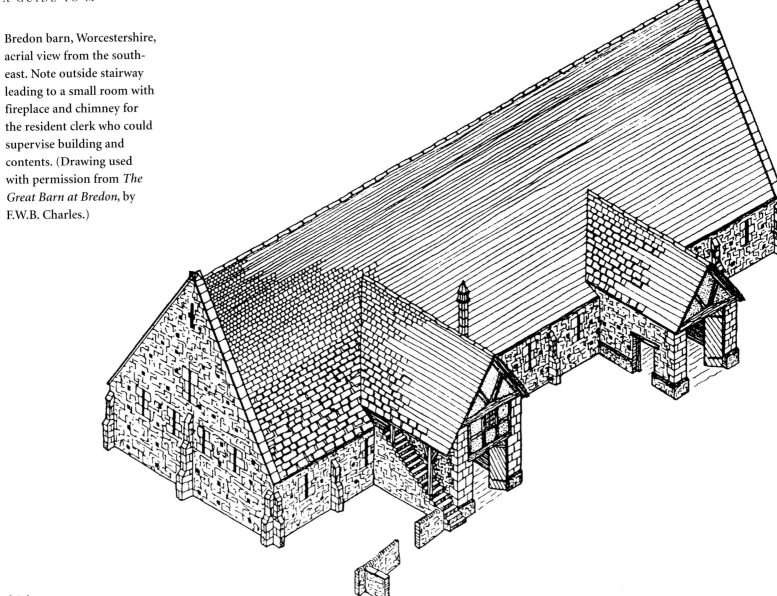

(Left) Bredon barn entrance from the opposite side showing the chimney for the fireplace in the clerk's room.

Bredon barn, showing clerk's room from the inside. Picture taken during restoration after a fire in 1980.

over his head in such a way that the lighter stick was brought down harshly on the stems of grain that were on the thrashing, or threshing, floor. The skill was to hit the stems just below the tops where the kernels had grown, thereby loosening them from the stems but without damaging them, so they would store well. Later, the grain would be taken to the miller to be ground into meal. The bundles of straw, after the grain had been thus removed, were then stacked up at the other end of the barn for later farm use.

The threshing of the grain took place in the late fall and winter, when farm labor was not in the fields. Thus, the barn was not only for storage, but also was an essential workplace, and was designed for this purpose as well.

Many of the barn doors opened into an enclosed porch that would have protected from the rain a waiting loaded wagon. An outer porch may also have had a second story that served as small but functional living quarters. A parish clerk sometimes lived in the room on the upper level of the main porch. He kept track of the tithes paid and provided security for the building and its valuable crop. The best example of this arrangement is the barn at Bredon, Worcestershire (see pages 8-9), where the priest's stone room included a tiny fireplace. From this, we can tell that he lived there year-round, though some would question the safety of having that fireplace so close to the combustible contents of the barn.

How to Find and Visit a Tithe Barn

Nearly all barns built during this four hundred-year period are similar in design, even though they may have been built three hundred years and three hundred miles apart. They are quite large, with single or double oversize doors located only on the sides and directly opposite one another. (The door opening at the end of the Great Coxwell barn is a recent alteration.) The roofs of all Tithe Barns slope at about a 60-degree angle and will be plain with no chimney. Because of this, when you first see a Tithe Barn—even from some distance—you can easily identify it as such.

To begin looking for barns, be sure to have a good road map of a scale no less than 5 miles to the inch, with a good index of all the towns and villages. A car rental agency map is not good enough. Most bookstores will have a selection of better maps.

When driving through the countryside in search of a particular barn, look first for the church tower or steeple, which is usually in the center of town. In small parishes, the Tithe Barn is likely to be located close to the parish church, so that the vicar could more easily keep track of tithe payments and distribution of tithed property. If you have difficulty finding a particular barn, stop at the town post office. People there usually know every building in the area.

If the barn you are visiting is located on private property, do not hesitate to enter the grounds, but make sure that you carefully close behind you any gate that you must open. Do not smoke. Slowly drive up to the house and park at some distance. You are probably being watched. Walk to the service door of the house, rather than the front door, ring the bell, and then step back at least ten feet from the door so that you can be seen from a side window. Your intention is to show that you are a nonthreatening visitor. It can also be helpful if you have a Canadian or American accent. Our experience has been that when you tell the residents that you are interested in Tithe Barns, they are generally very hospitable and helpful.

Travel with a pair of field glasses, because some of the things you will enjoy seeing will be located high up in the structure or on the roof of the barn.

Spying a barn across an open field and recognizing it as a Tithe Barn has always been a great thrill for us. To do this as a traveler, you will want to know something about the barns' historic background and their construction.

Society and Population

Let us begin with some basic facts about England in the post-Norman Conquest period. By 1066, the Christian Church, though still struggling with pagan traditions, was the dominant moral and social force in society. There was only one church, and it was the only way to avoid eternal damnation. Everybody belonged to the Church. Also, the royal government gave its official endorsement to the Church and was closely guided by Church principles. For example, the system of tithing was not only the way of life in the Church, but it was also enforced by the king.

In 1066, there were probably about one million people living in all of the area of Great Britain. The largest city, London, probably had only about 20,000 people. York and Winchester, two other concentrations of popu-lation, each likely had less than half that. This means that the great majority of the people lived in the countryside and gained their living from the land. However, most of them did not own that land; they were tenants of the lord of their estate, who held his right of ownership from the king. Their "cots," or houses, were clustered either close to the castle or manor house or in small groups to make a village. Nobody, not even the lord of the manor, lived in what we might call any type of luxury. Simple as their housing was, they did seem to have ample food.

By 1555, when Henry VIII dissolved the monasteries and established the Church of England, the population was probably about five million and might have been a great deal larger had it not been for the plagues, especially the Black Death of 1349. It is estimated that this disaster alone killed one third of the people and reduced the total population to about 2,500,000. This created a serious shortage of labor, with resulting social changes. Labor became more valuable and people were no longer tied to one estate. The "common man" enjoyed more power, more flexibility, more opportunities and a higher standard of living. The Guilds for skilled trades were very important at this time.

One agricultural change resulting from this shortage of labor was a movement away from grain farming toward raising large herds of sheep and the development of the wool industry. (This change comprises a whole field of research on its own and is not discussed further here.) But this shift in economy, along with the reduction in labor force, means that few Tithe Barns were built in the fifty years following the great plague.

Arable Land

The present-day visitor does not realize that much of the land once was covered by dense forest. Journey from place to place was accomplished by wooded trails. As a means of travel across the country, some of the Roman roads survived, but most of the trails went from village to village. Some of those ancient "Ways" are still in use, and are now identified as designated Public Foot Paths. Before a crop could be planted, then, trees had to be cleared. The suffix "ley" that appears on many town names, such as Durley and Oakley, means that originally they were located in a clearing in the forest.

There has been much discussion regarding the size of the typical medieval English farm. The farmland included woodlot, orchard, pasture, and arable land for grain crops. Architectural historians have been interested in establishing how much land had to be cleared to grow the amount of grain these Tithe Barns could hold. The Tithe Barns and farm at Cressing Temple have been extensively studied by John Hunter. In his report on Cressing Temple, he is able to reconstruct the early history of this tract based on old maps and existing land formations. The article is much too long to present here, but he speculates with good reason that in the 1300s, the arable land of the Cressing Temple farm was 521 acres. In addition to this, the farm had at least two hundred acres in woodland and other non-crop-raising land. As part of this study, Hunter refers to a research project done by John Weller in which Weller compares the productivity of the arable land to the size of the barns.[2]

Weller estimated that a field should produce about eighty sheaves of grain to the acre, each sheaf measuring two cubic feet. So 521 acres might produce 83,260 cubic feet of harvested grain and straw that would need to be brought into a barn. The two barns of Cressing Temple (one wheat and one barley) have 93,120 cubic feet of storage capacity with the central aisles left free. In the case of a bumper crop, the ends of the central aisles could also have been used. If we assume that Cressing Temple farmers were able to produce ten bushels of grain to the acre (current modern farming is producing eighty to one hundred bushels per acre), then 521 acres would have produced 5,210 bushels of grain. At five bushels per person per year, this would have fed one thousand people.

Timber Source

The standing forest covering the land—and in more settled areas, managed woodlots—also provided the essential building material for churches, barns, and dwellings. To a farmer, his woodlot was just as important as an arable field. All of his heating fuel as well as construction materials came from the lot. Woodlot care during this time involved the new technique of *pollarding*, which means that instead of harvesting a mature tree by cutting its trunk at the base, the tree was cut about six or eight feet above the base, thereby saving the strength of the roots and encouraging fast growth of new wood. When this new wood attained a useful diameter, it was then also harvested. Smaller-diameter timbers may have come from this second growth of pollarded trees.

The two barns at Cressing Temple, Essex. In the foreground, the Barley barn, circa 1130, and in the background, the Wheat barn, circa 1250.

Beech trees that have had their upper branches harvested by pollarding now show healthy second growth. (From Toys Hill Forest of the National Trust, Kent)

In the historical reports on Cressing Temple, there is also an article by Oliver Rackham on "Medieval Timber Economy."[3] He has carefully inventoried all the timbers in both the Wheat and the Barley Barns. For the Barley Barn, he calculates that there are 603 different timbers, made up of a total of 4,031 cubic feet of oak. Then he calculates the number of trees that were needed to produce that amount of lumber. He sorts the timbers by size, recognizing that the aisle posts needed a fully mature tree because of their size and length, but that many of the other timbers could have come either from branches of a mature tree or from younger growth.

Mr. Rackham puts all of this together and calculates that the Barley Barn needed the wood produced by 480 trees. Analyzing this need by the amount of space required for its growth in a woodlot, he comes to an interesting conclusion. He says, in part, "This means that a coppice-wood of 110 acres could have produced one Barley Barn every five years forever," or, stated another way, a barn that size required the growth of 12.2 acres of woodland for fifty years to produce the needed timber.[4]

This timber was obviously available in the 1200s, but by the reign of Henry VIII, the demand for wood for construction must have outgrown the supply. When King Henry started to create the first Royal Navy, he had to place restrictions on tree harvesting to make sure there would be enough timber to build his fighting ships.

Oak was the dominant wood used in all timber construction, although sometimes we see walnut and elm. As the preferred wood, oak was clearly more expensive, but oak is very strong and durable and, if kept dry, seems to last forever. As it ages, it becomes so hard that it cannot be worked as ordinary wood, but must be drilled and formed with power tools. You cannot hammer a regular nail into a dry oak beam. A hole must be drilled into oak with a steel drill and then plugged before it will accept even a screw.

Along with beech, walnut and elm, oak is one of the heavier English woods. To give an example, each of the fourteen posts in the barn at Coggeshall has as its dimensions fifteen and one-half inches by fifteen and one-half inches by twenty-two feet tall. This works out to contain 37.53 cubic feet of timber. Dried, reference books suggest, a post might weigh forty-five pounds per cubic foot.[5] But the builders were working with green timbers, which would be heavier. It is quite possible, then, that each finished post weighed a ton. But remember that the finished timber was cut from a log that, in rough form, could have weighed at least twice that. Felling the tree, stripping off the top branches, removing the bark—which was probably saved for tanning leather—and then removing the surplus wood to shape the final post must have been a tremendous task, all of which was required before the wood could be moved to the building site.

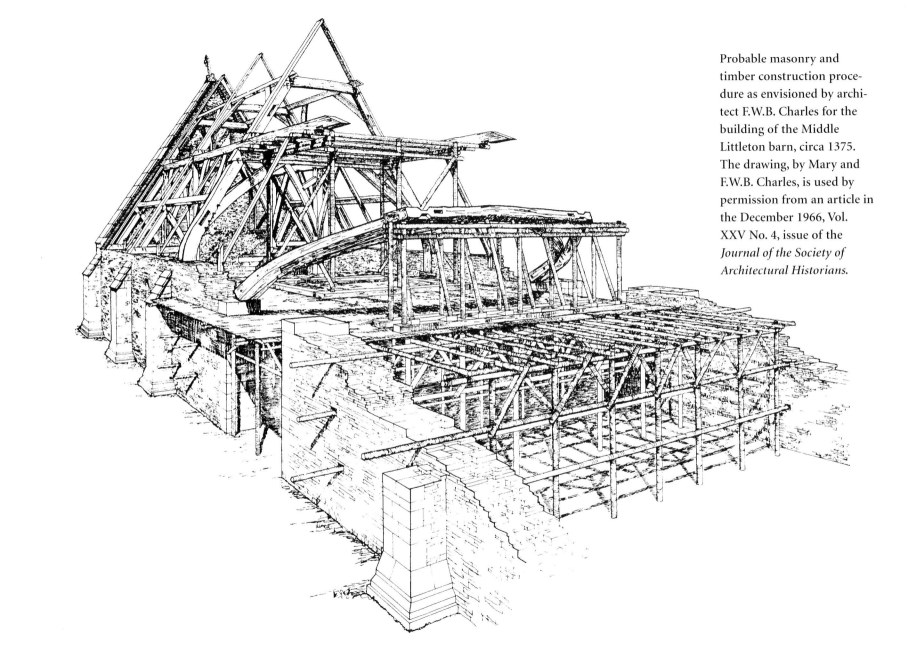

Probable masonry and timber construction procedure as envisioned by architect F.W.B. Charles for the building of the Middle Littleton barn, circa 1375. The drawing, by Mary and F.W.B. Charles, is used by permission from an article in the December 1966, Vol. XXV No. 4, issue of the *Journal of the Society of Architectural Historians.*

Barn Construction

Masonry

It is obvious that because of the difficulty of moving heavy objects, the builders of Tithe Barns would select their construction materials from local sources. Stone, the preferred material for walls, came from the local quarries, and the masons worked with what was available. In Devon and Cornwall it was granite, a very hard stone, good for durability but hard to work. In the eastern and central counties, there was limestone and sandstone, much easier to work, and in the Cotswold area, limestone has a beautiful, distinctive yellow color. Flint, the hardest of all, was found in East and West Sussex. And where stone was scarce, the builders made walls of wood, or wood framing filled in with brick, or with wattle and daub, a mixture of rods and branches filled in with clay or mud. In Norfolk, the Hales barn walls are made entirely of brick.

Probably building with stone was more expensive than building an all-wood barn. But in many cases, the stone walls made it possible to build a bigger barn with more storage capacity. The barn at Buckland Abbey has very tall masonry walls with no internal supports for the roof. The barn at Great Coxwell has seven-foot-tall masonry pillars supporting the timber posts for the roof, thereby producing that much more storage space.

As in a great church of similar size, where the walls of the crossing provide extra strength to the nave walls, in a Tithe Barn, the right-angle walls of the great side-door openings also provide stability. To save the use of stone, which was expensive, and still provide the necessary strength, masons built buttresses at the points where the timber trusses were attached to the walls. They also sometimes added corner buttresses just to play it safe, as at Buckland Abbey.

But in great contrast to the masonry work of a church, a Tithe Barn usually has no windows. For ventilation, the barn walls often have narrow eight-inch slits about three feet tall. On the inside, the masonry is splayed to let in the sunlight but keep out the rain. In some instances, such as the Glastonbury barn, a single set of openings like small church windows will have a religious significance, and in a few barns, the slit ventilation openings will be in the form of a cross. Occasionally a barn wall will have regularly spaced, small, four-inch square holes ("putlogs," again note the word) along the whole wall. These were used for the scaffolding that the masons needed for building the wall and the roof, and they are left in place for future use. Also, in a few barns, the masons built a dovecote into the end wall. We wonder who determined the ownership of the one-tenth tithe of the pigeon eggs collected.

Also in contrast with church masonry, Tithe Barns have very little decorative stonework on the exterior, and there is no decorative woodwork in the interior. The barn is strictly a functional structure.

Timber and Carpenters' Marks

Although there is no direct documentary evidence, it is quite probable that all the timbers for the barn structure were cut and fitted in a carpenter's yard located close to the source of the raw wood, and then the finished timbers were moved to the building site. The evidence of this building procedure is the carpenters' marks that appear at the joints of a truss. They can be found by the use of binoculars or, if the barn is full of hay or straw, by climbing up close to a joint. The markings are usually in Roman numerals and are the same number on each truss, but progress in number from one end of the barn to the other, indicating the sequence of the original construction.

Architect F.W.B. Charles, in his book on the restoration of the Bredon barn, reports two interesting refinements on the use of carpenters' marks. Not only is each truss numbered with Roman numerals sequentially, but also the timbers on the right half of the center line of each truss have the mark ^ added. Also, he found that IIII was used instead of IV for truss number four to avoid confusion since a poorly cut "V" might look like an "X."[6]

It is thought that the reason for these carpenters' marks is that the full truss, consisting of the two main

Carpenters' marks on beam joints, Black Notley barn, Essex.

posts and at least fifteen other timbers (as in the case of a truss in the barn at Great Coxwell), was first cut. Then the various joining joints were cut and fitted, and the actual truss was assembled on the ground to make sure it was accurate. The joints were then marked with the carpenters' marks and the truss disassembled, taken to the site, and there reassembled.[7] This would have been an efficient way to complete this work. But it is fun to speculate and to admire how skillful the carpenters were to be able to take the exact dimensions needed from the site of construction to the carpenter's yard with such control. For the barns like the ones at Cressing Temple, in which the sides that go to the ground are made of wood and are a part of the whole structure, an error of five or six inches in the total width of the barn could be adjusted. But for the barn at Middle Littleton, where the timbers fit into a separately constructed twelve-foot-high masonry wall, the dimensions over a thirty-foot width had to be accurate within an inch.

Structural Methods

When visiting the Houses of Parliament in London, you may be unaware of Westminster Hall (not to be confused with Westminster Abbey). Because the Parliament buildings are so imposing, and you are likely to be eager to see the beautiful interior, you may miss seeing Westminster Hall. Please stop and look.

In approximately 1097, red-haired King William Rufus erected on this site, as a part of his royal complex, Westminster Hall, probably the largest timber structure that had ever been built. Its dimensions were the same as the present hall, approximately 250 feet long by 75 feet wide. With masonry walls of the hall forty feet high, and the timber frame above that, the ridge of the roof is an incredible one hundred feet above the floor. The Norman invaders of England were committed to huge buildings, as evidenced by their construction at this same time of massive cathedrals at Durham, St. Albans, and Winchester. Archaeological study suggests that Westminster Hall, designed as a multipurpose meeting hall, had timber columns on both sides of a central aisle with parallel side aisles.[8] This created a structure very similar to a barn, but much larger. It is quite clear that this pioneering and daring building had a significant influence on later builders who needed barns to shelter and protect large amounts of farm products.

For a seemingly unrecorded reason, a new timber support system was placed in Westminster Hall in 1400. What has been recorded is that the roof was designed by Hugh Hertland for Richard II.[9] It is an example of an amazing carpentry design. In the opinion of some architectural experts, it is the greatest in the world.[10] Possibly the design was initiated because the king desired a full floor (approximately half-acre) without obstructions, and Hugh Hertland was faced with the problem of spanning an area wider than any oak tree was tall. He designed a truss system using a single hammerbeam and a collar arch. This is the roof support system that you see now when you look up.

It is strange that this ancient, unique, beautiful treasure has not attracted more visitor attention and is frequently overlooked. However, when the present Houses of Parliament were about to be built in 1840 after a disastrous fire, and the land for the area was to be cleared, it was decided—reportedly after much discussion—that Westminster Hall would stay in its own place, neither destroyed nor moved, and the new government buildings would be built adjacent.[11]

The original timber framing technique that was used in Westminster Hall in 1097 (more than nine hundred years ago) was what is now called "post and beam." It is this method of timber posts and trusses that has been used in many of the larger Tithe Barns. The drawing for the internal structure of the Great Coxwell barn on the next page shows this clearly.

Less common, but in some respects more beautiful, was the "cruck" structural method. Here, the carpenter carefully selected a tree with a curved trunk and a major branch, then sawed this trunk down the middle for the full length of the timber. When a series of opposing pairs were installed in the barn frame, they created not only an

open and unobstructed floor space, but also the beautiful appearance of an arched roof.

Most of the cruck framing was used in what is called the raised cruck method to span the space between high masonry walls, such as at Middle Littleton, Bradford-on-Avon, and Frocester. However, the barn at Leigh Court is quite different. Not only did the carpenters use the base cruck method with the timbers resting on a low foundation, but they also built the largest simple cruck structure in England and possibly the world. The eighteen timber blades that form the nine arches are from thirty-four to forty feet long. Research suggests that even a virgin forest of great oak trees would not be able to produce curved timber of sufficient diameter to be sawed in half. Thus, the blades are too long to have been obtained by the usual method of halving to produce a mirror image. Each blade is a single tree selected carefully so as to give a uniform appearance.

When we first visited the Leigh Court barn, it was still being used actively by the farmer, but it was in poor condition. Since then, the British Heritage has underwritten and supervised a complete restoration. It is open for inspection during the spring, summer, and early fall. (See pages 22 and 23.)

While the exteriors of Tithe Barns have in common a massive, steep, sloping roof over a building with large doors on the side walls, the interiors have individual differences that make every visit to a barn interesting. Why would the carpenters do this? When was it built? How did they put it all together?

The earlier barns, like the one at Coggeshall, were

How did tithe barns come to have this characteristic nave-and-side-aisle floor plan and high-backed shape? The floor plan clearly resembles the Roman basilica form, a roofed public space for various uses. In commercial use, the side aisles were good places for merchants' stalls while the public circulated in the middle space. The early Christians adapted the basilica form for churches.

A perspective drawing of the interior of the barn at Great Coxwell, Berkshire, looking northward, taken from a position outside the structure with the southern gable wall removed. (Used with permission from Horn and Born, *The Barns of the Abbey of Beaulieu*)

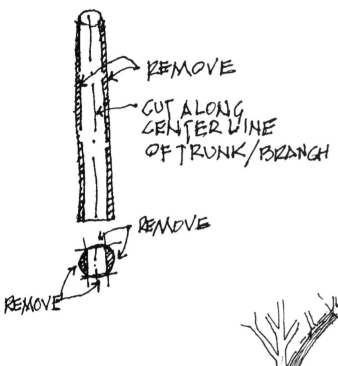

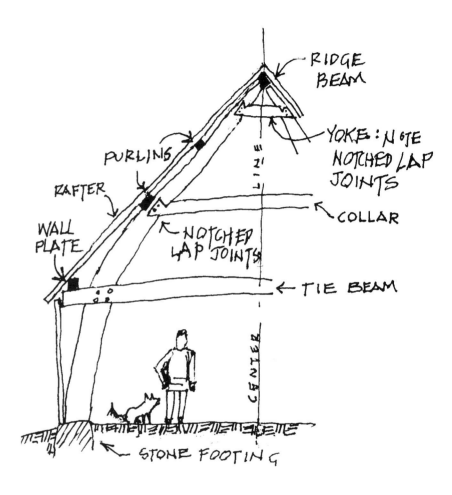

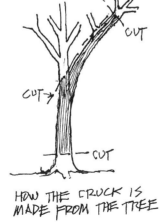

HOW THE CRUCK IS
MADE FROM THE TREE

(Right) How the cruck is
made from a tree.
(Above left) Two halves of
arched timber made from a
tree.
(Far Right) Full-cruck barn,
half section.

more simply built and contrast dramatically with barns like Buckland Abbey, built two hundred years later, with its buttressed stone walls and sixty-foot-high roof. At Coggeshall, the great timber posts sit directly on the barn floor and are slightly tapered, like the tree they came from, as they rise toward the roof. At Buckland Abbey, there are no columns; the side walls were set close enough that the roof trusses span from wall to wall. The builders must have had good reason, but now it is hard to imagine why they built the roof sixty feet high. Certainly it would

Leigh Court barn, Worcestershire, interior before restoration.

have been difficult to fill that barn even three-fourths full with unthreshed grain.

The side walls of some barns were of timber, and the roof came down very close to the ground. The two barns at Cressing Temple in Essex are good examples.

Sometimes the side walls were made of timber framing, and the spaces between the uprights were in-filled with brick, as at High Roding. Other times, the spaces were made of timber panels or woven sticks, against which clay or plaster could be applied to make a solid wall.

Leigh Court barn, exterior after restoration.

The drawing on page 16 shows the imagined construction procedure for the barn at Middle Littleton, with its masonry walls. However, if the building had no stone walls, the procedure for construction would have been quite different. Just as at Middle Littleton, the major posts had to be fully prepared, with all the needed joints and the related joining set of timbers and braces. Then we can imagine that by using lifting and guy-line ropes attached to an auxiliary

(Left) Detail, brick infill, High Roding barn, Essex. Note the different brick patterns in each panel.

(Above) Exterior, Leigh Court barn, Worcestershire. Here the wall has three different types of construction: clapboard, brick infill, and woven sticks designed to hold clay.

Exterior, High Roding barn, Essex, circa 1488.

[25]

pole, or a set of poles, the builders were able to get an initial post, and finally a set of four posts, pulled up to a vertical position. Then the builders must have assembled horizontal beams and braces to create a stable unit. With that in place, the rest of the columns could be erected more easily.

Over time and with experience, the builders improved the setting of the main columns by using lateral sill timbers, or small stone plates, as a base. At Great Coxwell, the aisle posts are set on top of seven-foot stone pillars. Because the end grain of the timber posts would be exposed to rot from dampness rising in the stone beneath, they inserted a square bolster pad of wood between them, so that any moisture would follow the horizontal grain of the pad and evaporate at the ends. This technique has evidently worked very well, because the pads and the columns are still there.

Cressing Temple Barley barn showing vertical columns resting on timber ground sills.

Masonry column in Great Coxwell. Horizontally placed oak block evaporates moisture rising from masonry thereby avoiding possible rot to the base of the timber column.

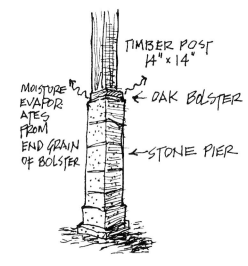

TIMBER POST 14" x 14"

MOISTURE EVAPORATES FROM END GRAIN OF BOLSTER

← OAK BOLSTER

← STONE PIER

Timber Joints

The highly developed skill of the carpenters is particularly evident on inspection of the joints the carpenters devised when two or more timbers were brought together. These craftsmen understood very well the structural requirements of a strong building, and they were ingenious in the way they worked with the materials at hand. Fortunately for us, Cecil A. Hewett, in his book, *English Historic Carpentry,* presents his findings in graphic form. To whet your appetite for further study, we present here only three different types of joints, each serving a different purpose. The strength of these joints was critical.

The first type is the scarf joint. This was used in any beam that would run horizontally the length of the barn. Because no tree was tall enough to provide a single beam long enough, the beam had to be created from timbers that were joined end-to-end. The joint needed to provide only longitudinal stability. Joints found in early buildings are very simple, while those found in later buildings are more complicated, thus providing a clue for rough dating of the construction of the barn. An early and a late scarf joint are shown.

The barn roof is not only heavy, but because of its size, it is also subjected to great horizontal pressure in a strong wind. Therefore, the second major type of joint is the lap joint for triangular wind braces. These occur all over the barn. To function correctly, they must resist both tension and compression. A design to resist compression into the joint is simple, but note the notch on the end of each wind brace where it is attached to the

Early halved scarf joint (1180-1200) with faced pegs used for top plate. Lacks strength; all resistance to tension is in pegs.

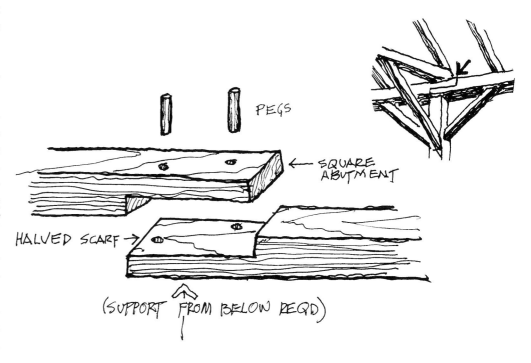

PEGS

SQUARE ABUTMENT

HALVED SCARF →

(SUPPORT FROM BELOW REQD)

One variation on scarf joint. Stiff and strong in all directions. Cressing Wheat Barn c. 1250.

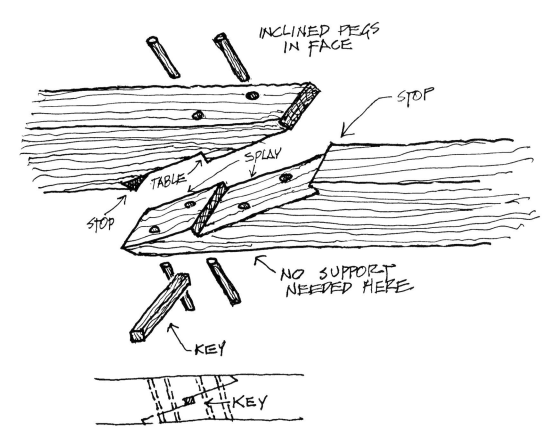

timber, designed to resist external tension that might pull the beam out of the joint. Some of these notches are hidden, not to be devious but because the notch is stronger when it occurs in the center of the timber. The drawings on the next page show both of these arrangements.

The third type of joint occurs at the top of a support column. This column transfers the weight of the roof to the floor as its main task, but in addition it supports the base of a triangular truss that gives the whole structure stability. Therefore, the horizontal beams that extend in three or four directions from the top of the column must be securely fixed. The dovetailed lap joint is designed to provide this security, as can be seen by analyzing the drawing on page 30. In a standing barn, it is impossible to see this clever creation, so our thanks go to Mr. Hewett for providing this research.[12] These joints also provide clues as to the approximate date of construction of the barn.

To secure the timbers together at their joints, a hole was drilled into both the main timber and the joining timber to receive an oak peg. The peg was purposely not cut perfectly round, so that when driven into the hole, it would seize the sides of the hole and make a tighter fit. Sometimes these pegs are called trunnels, which sounds very similar to "tree nails." This technique for fastening heavy construction timbers was used right up until the twentieth century, and is found in most American barns, although few of these barns are made out of oak.

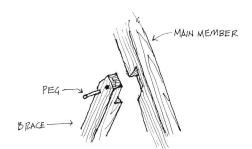

Simple lap joint, circa 1000, for brace to main member. Joint is good in compression, weak in tension or pulling.

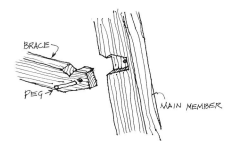

Improved lap joint, circa 1130, using a notch, which will resist compression and tension. Sometimes the notch is hidden inside the main timber, which gives the joint even greater strength.

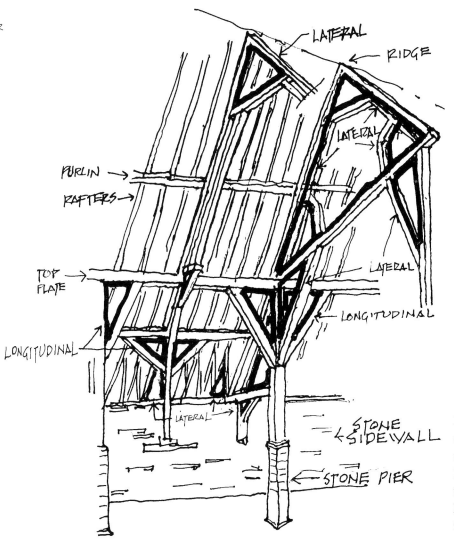

Drawing showing a partial section of the timber framing of the Great Coxwell Barn. Heavy black lines show the triangular braces resisting longitudinal and lateral forces that the barn is subjected to by heavy winds.

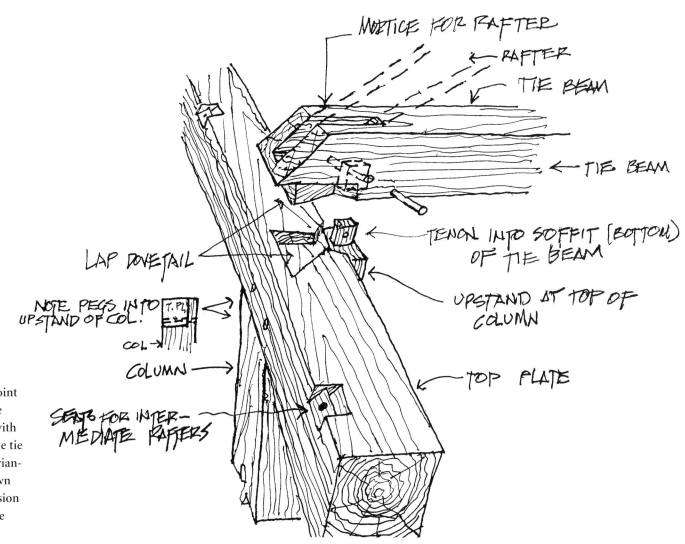

MORTICE FOR RAFTER

RAFTER

TIE BEAM

TIE BEAM

TENON INTO SOFFIT (BOTTOM) OF TIE BEAM

LAP DOVETAIL

NOTE PEGS INTO UPSTAND OF COL.

7. PL.

COL →

COLUMN →

UPSTAND AT TOP OF COLUMN

TOP PLATE

SEATS FOR INTER-MEDIATE RAFTERS

The most complicated joint of all. Here the top of the column is tightly fitted with both the top plate and the tie beam. Other necessary triangular braces are not shown in order to reduce confusion in the diagram. Please see other diagrams.

Painting

Because most American barns require paint for their preservation, we asked how English barns were painted. They are not. Evidently, the sap from a green oak tree bleeds to the surface and then hardens to give permanent protection, and the wood of the barn does not require paint.

Roofing

While there are a few thatched barns, most Tithe Barns are roofed with ceramic tile or slate. Thatching was used where there was ample local material and probably cost less than a slate or tile roof, but it did not last as long. There is plenty of evidence of ceramic tile having been made by the Romans during their occupation, so it is not surprising to find that Tithe Barn builders also made ceramic tiles for their buildings.

Middle Littleton, Worcestershire. The new roof in 1979. Unfortunately, the original tapestry of colors of the new and old slates has faded. Note the stone finial at the end of the ridge. According to folklore, this is to keep away evil spirits.

Middle Littleton, Worcestershire. During restoration in 1978, all of the stone slates were removed from the roof and checked for quality. Here the good slates have been sorted for size. The smaller ones, six to eight inches long, are stacked in rows at the left, and the larger sizes, sixteen and seventeen inches, are to the right.

However, where there was a regional supply of field-stone or slate for shingles, this seems to have been the preferred roofing material.

For both the tile and slate roof, the hanging technique is quite similar. Long wooden battens, about one by two inches, are attached horizontally to the rafters about six to eight inches apart along the whole surface of the roof. Then each tile, or slate, is hung on a batten by the use of a half-inch-diameter wooden peg about four inches long, inserted in a hole at the top of the shingle. (A modern adaptation is to use a peg made out of aluminum.)

Middle Littleton, Worcestershire. The underside of the barn roof. The field-stone slates hang on wooden battens with a peg. Originally the peg was made of wood. Now it is a thick aluminum nail. Note especially in the center of the photograph the slate with the empty hole. Evidently the roof restorer felt the old hole was weak, and a new hole was made.

This technique has the important advantage of not only shedding the water, but also providing a roof that is a good ventilator. Beause the grain was brought into the barn while it was still green, it was essential that the drying of the grain be enhanced by good ventilation. When you walk into a slate-covered barn on a sunny day, you will see a roof full of pinpoints of light. Still, that roof on a rainy day will shed the water.

Slates, or tiles, are heavy. This is one of the reasons that the internal timber structure is so sturdy. It is esti-mated that the roof surface of the Great Coxwell barn, which is only average in size when compared with other barns, is 12,800 square feet.[13] If you estimate that slate or tile weighs about ten pounds per square foot of coverage, you will find that the total weight of its roofing material comes to sixty-four tons. To give an example of how heavy this is, the largest tanker truck fully loaded with 10,000 gallons of oil weighs just under fifty tons.

Because the size of the hand-made tiles used for roof-ing is uniform, the hanging of the tiles on the roof is also uniform. However, fieldstone slates are quite different. They are found in sizes from six to eighteen inches long. This requires a different hanging method. First, the slates are sorted by size. Then the battens are placed to accept slates that are uniform in size. The small, or shorter, ones are placed at the top of the roof, where presumably there is less run-off, with the sizes increasing toward the bottom edge of the roof, where the run-off is the greatest. The casual observer will not notice this, but it becomes readily apparent if you use binoculars to inspect the top of the roof.

Restoration and Repair

In the period that we have been investigating English Tithe Barns, we are aware of five that have received extensive help.

When we first visited the Coggeshall barn, it was a shambles. As the picture shows, much of the tile of the roof was coming off, the timbers on the ends were rotting and falling down, and the barn itself was about to collapse. We will not attempt to relate the historic effort on the part of many interested people who felt the barn was a treasure (a visit to the barn now will supply you with the story), but their success is dramatically evident when you compare the "Before" and "After" pictures of the barn.

Coggeshall, Essex. This is what we found when we came to Coggeshall in 1979. My notes made at that time say we believed the barn to be beyond repair, a remnant of what was originally a fine barn. Later we read of efforts being made for its restoration in the publications of the Society for the Protection of Ancient Buildings. We then learned of its completion and finally of its transfer to the National Trust.

One of the interesting facts that surfaced when the Coggeshall barn was restored is the observation that the tapered aisle columns suggest that this barn is possibly the oldest complete barn in England. It is now part of the National Trust properties and has a good historic display inside for visitors.

On one of our early trips, we had visited the Middle Littleton barn. It was sheltering two great circular silos that were receiving and storing grain, which had been dried by machinery also located in the barn. It was doing the same job of protecting foodstuff that it had been designed for six hundred years earlier. However, it obviously was in need of additional care. The National Trust provided this. We were there one summer when the whole roof was stripped of all slate and battens and then covered with a great transparent plastic sheet. It gave a perfect opportunity for photographs of the structural beams of the roof. The pictures on the next page reveal two interesting details about the timber construction. First, the use of a double-tie beam as part of the cruck truss, and second, the quite noticeable use of crooked timbers, suggesting that the master carpenter had a limited choice of oak trees to work with.

The renewed Coggeshall Barn. In 1996 we returned to find this beautiful building fully restored and under protective care, a wonderful example of what can be done when people get together to solve an important problem.

Middle Littleton, Worcestershire. During restoration in 1978, all the stone slates on the roof were taken off and the roof was covered with plastic sheets in order for the farmer to continue to use the barn. This gave a perfect opportunity to photograph the oak timbers. Note that these timbers are not as straight as usually found in other barns, suggesting that the carpenters did not have as good a selection of trees in the area when they were building. The double tie beam truss is an unusual feature of this barn.

This visit during restoration also gave us insight into the procedure necessary for restoring the roof. The fieldstone roof slates were sorted by size on the ground before they were restored to the building, and new slates were being prepared. On the ground, they looked dull and uninteresting, but the multitude of shades of color in the freshly installed roof made a beautiful pattern. Unfortunately, time has dulled the colors.

We had first visited the Bredon barn when it was full of baled straw, so full that you could not even get in the big side door. A few years later, the straw accidentally caught fire and burned all its contents. We made a visit

Bredon barn, Worcestershire, immediately after the fire in 1980. (From *The Great Barn of Bredon,* by F.W.B. Charles. Photograph by his son Martin Charles. Used by permission.)

(Right) Interior of Bredon barn, Worcestershire. F.W.B. Charles, supervising restoration architect, showing Bonnie Griswold some of the details of the reconstruction.

soon after the fire. The roof, of course, was gone, but surprisingly many of the oak timbers were only badly charred. The National Trust, who were the owners of the barn, elected to rebuild. We had previously met Freddie and Mary Charles, architects who specialized in buildings of this period. Mr. Charles was in charge of the restora-

tion. He invited us to see the Bredon barn while it was under repair. We were amazed by how many of the original timbers could be salvaged. The picture shows how new wood was fitted and joined to old, reminding us of how a dentist fits a new crown to the top of an old tooth. The barn is again in use.

The fourth barn that has benefited from restoration care is Leigh Court, the largest "cruck-built" structure in Britain. It has recently had important repairs provided by British Heritage and should now be ready for the twenty-first century. The barn has no aisle posts. The roof is supported by great curved oak timbers that are themselves supported by a masonry sill, producing a large floor area with no columns, big enough for a tennis court.

The fifth barn is at Widdington, just south of Cambridge in Essex. When we first visited, it was in very poor condition with most of the roof gone, and the great timbers were held in position by internal steel pipe scaffolding. For some reason, its restoration was delayed, but we understand that it has now been completed.

All five of these barns are well worth a visit.

(Left) Bredon barn, Worcestershire. Interior after restoration. (Photo by Martin Charles. Used with permission)

Bredon barn, Worcestershire. Many of the great oak beams of the barn were charred only on the outside half inch, which did not damage the integrity of its strength. However, some other beams were destroyed only at the joining area. For these beams, new oak was fitted, glued, and pegged much the way a dentist attaches a crown to a damaged tooth. Here are two beams being refitted.

Conversions

With the development this past fifty years of more efficient farm machinery and greatly improved farming techniques, the method of producing food on English farms has changed greatly. This means that the use of farm buildings has changed also, and the original use of the Tithe Barn has disappeared. Farm machinery can be stored in a low metal shed that is much less expensive to maintain. Harvested grain and similar produce, such as

Conversion of barn into a single dwelling.

potatoes and beets, are frequently hauled right to the processor rather than being stored.

All this means that many barns in recent years were abandoned and torn down. A few were converted to some other use. Sometimes the barn became a gymnasium for a school (Sturry), a meeting place for the community with a stage at one end (Burton-on-the-Hill), a restaurant full of Old World ambience (Garstang), or a place for wedding receptions and parties (Prestbury). Some conversions were made into dwellings, but this is difficult. A barn is big, and it has few windows. The conversion results in a compromise. However, one conversion at Cerne Abbas, with the

Cerne Abbas, Dorset. The south end of this barn has in it a three-story dwelling The balance of the barn is used for agricultural purposes.

(Below) Preston Plucknett, Somerset. The street side of this barn has been restored to its original condition by a building contractor.

Preston Plucknett, Somerset. The building contractor has converted the interior of the barn into an excellent supply warehouse which, because of the barn's size, can handle all kinds and sizes of equipment.

dwelling in one end of the barn and the remaining half left untouched, seemed to us to be very well done.

At Preston Plucknett, the south facade of the barn facing the street has been preserved beautifully. But as you go around the barn to the other side where the owner, who is a building contractor, has his storage yard, the barn has been ingeniously converted to a great warehouse, where even the biggest items find ample space. The fine barn at Glastonbury has quite appropriately been made the center for a farm museum.

In many ways, England has done a remarkable job in protecting and preserving her historic buildings. We can only hope that more of the still-remaining Tithe Barns will be included in this effort.

Dating of Construction

There are different methods for dating English churches and barns. When building or expanding or repairing a church, it was evidently important to use the latest "style," whether it be Saxon, Norman, Early Gothic or Perpendicular. We do not think they had those names for their particular current "style," but the master mason clearly knew what was going on in western Europe and gave his patrons the latest. The result is that many times a church will have examples of two or three styles within one structure. Consequently, it is possible to date a church, or parts of a church, by its style of masonry, within a fifty- or seventy-five-year period.

But this is not the case with a barn, for which utility was more important than style. During this period, farming techniques changed very little, and the design of a barn also remained the same. Even the masonry walls of a barn are rarely helpful in revealing the date of construction. One exception to this is found in the corbels of the barn at Great Coxwell. They have been examined by architects Walter Horn and Ernest Born, who found a parallel comparison to other corbels in a church building with known construction dates. From this, they conclude an early-thirteenth-century construction date for the Great Coxwell barn.[14]

The most accurate source of information for the date of construction of a barn would be ancient contemporary documents. In some few cases, these do exist. Considerable research has been done from original documents for the barns at Cressing Temple, for instance, so their construc-

tion dates are quite specific. However, for most barns, we must rely on the evidence at hand. The research done by Cecil A. Hewett, published in his book *English Historic Carpentry,* is probably the best resource. He has analyzed carpentry methods as revealed in present buildings, especially in the evolution of joint design, and has reported on their probable dates. He has found, however, that carpenters were not as likely as masons to use the latest "style," so that sometimes the "latest" was not being used.

Recent technical research has produced two new sources for dating. One is called carbon dating, which analyzes a small segment of wood under intense heat. This can be accurate to within fifty to seventy-five years

Carved stone corbel serving as a base for timber truss in masonry wall of Great Coxwell Barn. Also note putlog hole used to hold scaffolding.

(plus or minus). A second developing method is to compare a sample of the tree rings with a known set of rings. Sometimes this can give an accurate date as to when the tree was felled, leaving the assumption that it was used in construction soon after. However, because of differences in climatic conditions by year in different parts of Europe, it is sometimes difficult to develop a reliable local test sample against which comparisons can be made.

Another complication for accurate dating comes from the fact that it was common practice to recycle old timbers in the construction of a new barn. Thus, a barn built in 1450 might well have timbers from a barn built in 1200. Sometimes these older timbers can be spotted, because they may have mortice cavities cut into them that are not now being used and have no relevance to their present location.

In some instances there are stones set into the wall of a barn, giving the initials of the owner and a date. These may not be accurate for the date of construction, because they may have been added at a time of restoration.

The Great Tithe Barn of Cholsey, Berkshire

It may seem strange to report on a Tithe Barn that disappeared in 1815, but this barn was remarkable in many ways and deserves a place in this story. Fortunately, just before it was dismantled, its uniqueness was recognized and the engraving below, as well as an architect's drawing of the plan of the trusses and the floor, did survive.

First, the barn was remarkable because it was probably not only the largest barn ever built in England, but also the largest structure of its type ever built in Europe. It was 303 feet long, 54 feet wide, and 51 feet tall. The roof area would have been 30,770 square feet (nearly three-fourths of an acre) and was covered with an estimated 230,000 tiles.

The late barn of Cholsey, Berkshire. (From *Gentleman's Magazine*, February 1816, taken from an article by Walter Horn in the *Journal of the Society of Architectural Historians*, March 1963)

Second, the barn roof was supported on thirty-four stone pillars (seventeen on each side), each one three feet square and thirty-one feet tall. The master builder probably used masonry columns, because for a building this large, he would have had difficulty first finding thirty-four oak trees tall enough, then preparing these trees for use, and finally putting them in place. A few barns in northern Europe use masonry pillars, but rarely in England. However, in a very modified way, seven-foot stone columns are used in the Great Coxwell barn. This construction method does enlarge the capacity of the barn, but even so, the internal capacity of the barn at Cholsey was more than two and a half times greater than Great Coxwell's.

As you would expect, the barn at Cholsey had doors opposing each other on the long side of the barn, but four on each side rather than two.

The date of construction of the Cholsey barn is difficult to determine. Walter Horn, in his article on the barn, suggests a fourteenth-century date based on other similar construction.[15]

If the Cholsey Barn were still standing, what an exciting scene it would make!

The Great Barn formerly at Cholsey, Berkshire. Interior perspective reconstruction. (Drawing by Ernest Born.)

Frocester Barn, Gloucester
Built 1284-1306
183 feet long
Part of a large farm building complex and still in active use.

(Above left) East end showing related buildings. (Left) Roof repair. (Above) Interior roof framing.

A Brief History of Tithing

TITHING GENERALLY REFERS TO A SYSTEM of paying a share (one-tenth) of the agricultural produce of one's land, livestock, and labor to the church for its support. This system evolved to its greatest effectiveness during the four hundred years following the Norman invasion of England in 1066. In this period, tithing was the law of the land, promulgated not only by the church, but also by royal decree.

The history of this development is a long one, and quite parallel to the history of the development of Christianity. We begin with the Bible where in Genesis 28:20-22, we find this reference:

> Thereupon Jacob made this vow: If God will be with me, if he will protect me on my journey and give me food to eat and clothes to wear, and I will come back safely to my father's house, the Lord shall be my God, and this stone which I have set up as a sacred pillar shall be the house of God. And all that thou givest me, I will without fail allot a tenth part to thee.

Certainly as a method of supporting the religion of the Hebrews, which in a sense was also their government, this was an accepted and widespread procedure. It has been suggested by some historians that this special offering to God is not a special Hebrew concept, however, and that similar acts of thanks for help in the performance of difficult tasks have been made by other Eastern Mediterranean groups as well.

As we go further into the Bible, references to tithes become more specific. In Leviticus 27:30-32 is the following:

> Every tithe on land, whether from grain or from the fruit of a tree, belongs to the Lord; it is holy unto the Lord. If a man wishes to redeem any of his tithe, he shall pay its value increased by one-fifth. Every tenth creature that passes under the counting rod shall be holy to the Lord; this applies to all tithes of cattle and sheep. There shall be no inquiry whether it is good or bad, and no substitution. If any substitution is made, then both the tithe animal and its substitute shall be forfeit as holy; it shall not be redeemed.

Other references to tithing in the Old Testament are in Numbers 18:26-28, Deuteronomy 12:17-19 and 12:22-29, Chronicles 31:5, 31:6 and 31:12, and Malachi 3:8 and 3:12. These outline more specifically the items subject to tithe, the distribution of tithes, and the penalty for not tithing. The reference to tithing in the New Testament is quite different and reflects the revolutionary teaching of Jesus. He does not question the system, but he says that tithing alone is not enough. In Luke 11:42 is the following: "Alas for Pharisees! You pay tithes of mint and rue and every garden-herb, but you have no care for justice and the love

(Opposite) Braemore, St. Mary's Church, Hampshire, containing some Saxon masonry, indicating that part of the original church may have been built before 1000.

of God. It is these you should have practiced, without neglect of the others."

The Christian church, as it spread through southern Europe during the first three or four centuries after Christ, left no record of the use of tithing for the support of those early missionaries. By the beginning of the fifth century, there is evidence that both the Greek and Latin churches claimed the support of tithing, but it was a moral and religious obligation rather than a legal one.

A decree of Pope Galasius (492-496) must have been written because of a need to be more specific about the use of tithes or "revenues" for the church:

> The revenues of every church and the obligations are to be divided into four portions: one for the Bishop, a second for the clergy, a third for the poor, and a fourth for the fabric of the church; and let the good repairs of the sacred buildings demonstrate the Bishop's care for them, and let witnesses of the best credit testify for faithfulness in giving to the poor their portion.

By the year 787, Charlemagne, King of the Franks and Roman Emperor, ordained by imperial law that each person shall pay tithes, "and they may be dispensed according to the order of the Bishop."

But for purposes of this study, we need now to report on the development of tithing not in Europe, but in England. In Britain, there were organized Christian outposts by 314 A.D. This is confirmed by the signatures of the British representatives who were attendees of the Council of Arles.

By 597, when Saint Augustine came from Rome to found a Christian settlement at Canterbury, the spread of Christianity was extensive. Further north, Saint Columbo had come from Ireland to found a church at Iona. There were also groups in Wales, and Saint Augustine found a group already established in Canterbury. Each group seemed to be based on an independent authority, so much so that the Council of Whitby was called in 664 essentially to determine the proper time for the celebration of Easter. However, the regional independence of each group was such that even after a common agreement determined at Whitby, the local groups followed their traditional calendars for yet another century.

The Council of Whitby did mark, however, the beginning of the effort of the Roman Church to establish a unified church in Britain. When Theodore of Tarsus came to Britain in 668, he organized the church into more formalized groups with levels of authority and territories of responsibility called townships and parishes. But even then, tithing seems to have been voluntary and to have been paid by those who felt the greatest need for the strength and services of the church. Some evidence of this comes from the fact that conferences were held in 787 in both the north of Britain, under Ethelwald, King of Northumbria, and in the south of Britain, under Offa, King of Mercia. The delegates sent a report to Pope Adrian I saying, "Tides be paid in Full." How or whether this decree was enforced has not been historically determined.

By 901, under Edward the Elder, the obligation of the tithe was established by law, including a penalty for nonpayment. By 928, in a Grand Council, King Athelstane issued a royal injunction for tithes as follows: "I, King

Athelstane, by the advice of my Archbishop and Bishops, strictly enjoin all my reeves, in the name of God and all his Saints, to pay the tithes, both cattle and corn, out of my lands." Then, after quotations from both the Old and New Testaments he added, ". . . and let us remember it is threatened in the same books, that if we will not pay our tithes, the nine parts shall be taken from us, and the tenth part only shall be left us."

By the end of the tenth century, it becomes difficult to trace the evolution of the British tithing system by dates, because tithing developed rapidly as Britain prospered and the influence of the Church became greater. The laws became more specific on the subject of special days of the year when certain tithes were paid, and in the definitions of which goods were subject to tithes, listing wheat, flocks, goats, butter, cheese, bees, pigs, milk, fisheries, gardens, mills, etc. How the tithe master took care of such perishable produce as bees and milk is not revealed.

Furthermore, there were laws to determine which church was entitled to tithes, because sometimes the lord of the manor would designate the fruit of his land located in a distant parish for the support of a church in his own area. In some cases, distant lands were given outright for the support of a particular monastery, and this caused jurisdictional questions.

There were also questions of whether the tithes of a particular area were owed to the principal church of the diocese for the bishop to distribute or whether they went to the local church, and, if so, whether the local church had to share a portion of the tithe with the mother church. Under the laws of Edgar, circa 970, the assign-

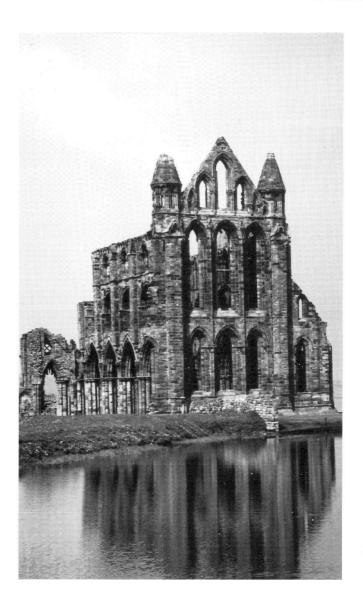

Ruin of Whitby Abbey, North Yorkshire, built circa 1150.

ment of tithes was dependent on the class of church in the area, with the divisions as follows:

A. Older, or principal, churches;
B. Churches with burial grounds which lords might have on the grounds of their manors;
C. Churches without burial grounds.

The churches of Class A received the major part of the tithe, but if there were churches of other classes in the same diocese, they shared smaller amounts.

The time for the payment of tithes was determined as follows: Whitsuntide (the seventh Sunday after Easter) for the tithe of cattle, and Martinmas (November 11) for the payment of earth's fruits. The king's and bishop's reeves together with the mass-priest of the principal church were to go to the defaulter and take the whole of his produce. The tithe due the principal church was then taken, and the defaulter given back one-tenth.

Just before the Norman invasion, there seems to have developed a period of laxness in the enforcement of tithing. This may have been due to internal conflicts that were weakening the nobility, or because the churches had become quite prosperous and careless in enforcement. This observation is supported by the fact that the detailed inventory of English property in the Domesday Book, prepared under the reign of William I in 1085, rarely mentions the right of tithe, even though real endowments and revenues of the clergy are listed and valued.

By the reign of Henry II (1154-1189), payment of tithes became so slack that Pope Alexander III interfered to reestablish the practice. By the time of Henry III (1216-1272), the full force of the law was applied to all lands to pay tithes to the parish or to the mother church.

More precise laws were still required, though, because there were occasions when the lords of the land chose to direct their tithes as they thought best. Many monasteries had been founded by the year 1200, mostly from the appropriations of large landowners. Each lord considered his monastery his own private endeavor, and he had great influence in the selection of the clergy. The result produced not only great inequality in the distribution of wealth within the church, but also serious questions about who was responsible for administration. This problem of confused authority resulted in situations in which the lord of the land felt he still retained ownership of the church and the land related to it, and occasionally made a sale of it for other purposes.

As the importance of the tithing system grew for its support of the monasteries and the churches, so did it become more complicated. Definitions of what was subject to tithe became more precise, and the system became invasive in an effort not to miss any opportunity for revenue. The vicar was entitled to receive what were called the "Small Tithes," and the rector the "Great Tithes." The application of this distinction seems to be regional, but, in general, Great Tithes were corn, grain, hay and wood. The other produce of the land was considered Small Tithes. This got very complicated, however. For example, hops grown in a field were Great, and hops grown in a garden were Small. Fish caught for resale were Great, but fish caught for personal use were Small. And what about the miller, since most of the grain that he processed was not his own, but that of local farmers? He tithed his tenth of the portion of the grain he withheld for his services.

Along with this system of collecting revenue for the church from the fruit of the land, there developed a parallel system of paying Mortuaries. Originally, they were voluntary payments made to the minister on the death of any of his parishioners. By the time of Henry III, they had become regularized. The payment was usually the best animal in the dead person's flock, a very significant payment for most farmers, since their flocks were small.

For many reasons, by the time of the reign of Henry VIII (1509-1547), the church, while internally very strong and wealthy, was losing its influence over the people of Britain. The oppression of the tithing system was probably a contributing factor. But a study of history for that period indicates it was much more complex than that. Certainly the church no longer had the general support of the people, or Henry VIII would not have been able to proceed with his plan of seizing the monasteries. In addition, it is true that he needed money for the building of the navy; it is true that he had difficulty with the Pope in Rome when he needed to change wives to try to have a son (fortunately he did not succeed, because his daughter eventually became Queen Elizabeth); and it is true that England was becoming a power unto itself. Henry VIII could not tolerate having to rule with an outside authority, such as the Pope, controlling his bishops. Henry VIII's seizure of all monasteries and his appointment of himself as the head of the Church of England produced a great change in the English church.

When the "Dissolution" was over, the government had appropriated all of the monasteries, which amounted to more than one third of the parish churches. The property of the monasteries was then sold to laypersons. This clearly complicated the tithing system, but for the remaining churches it continued, though on a declining basis.

For the purposes of this study of barns, we have not pursued the development of tithes after the Dissolution, nor have we included any barns built after that period. Barns were built after the Dissolution, and they were probably used for the storage of tithes, but we have felt their contribution to this field of history and architecture was minimal.

This is a condensed report on a very complicated subject. It is a bit like trying in the year 3000 to report on the development of the U. S. Federal income tax system during the second half of the twentieth century.

Buckland Abbey Tithe Barn, Devon, circa 1300. From an original drawing by C. Robinson of Plymouth England, done in 1992 at the request of the Exeter Hospital in Exeter, New Hampshire, in appreciation for service as a trustee by James W. Griswold.

Suggestions for Visiting a Tithe Barn

WHEN YOU SPOT AT SOME DISTANCE WHAT looks like a Tithe Barn, slow down, adjust your mental time frame, and become a member of medieval society.

If what you saw really turns out to be a barn, don't drive right up to the barn, but stop and park 100 yards away. Look around at the surrounding countryside; eliminate from your vision any more modern buildings that seem to intrude. Include in your vision a timber-framed house, if there is one, and the parish church. Also include in your imagination miscellaneous farm animals, certainly a dog, and men, women and children, clothed in crude, heavy work garments.

Do not go directly into the barn. Rather, walk all around the outside. Think about why it was sited where it is. Does the land look like good farmland? Was there a river close by to help with transportation? Then inspect the foundation: is it stone or wood? If it is stone, it is probably original; if wood, it has probably been repaired and replaced many times, but there may still be fragments of the original.

Look at the roof. If it is thatched, you know it is not original, but it still may be 100 years old. At the ridge line, there may be a pattern still showing the thatcher's trim, which serves as his signature. The locals know who he was. If the roof is tile or fieldstone, it is probably older, but also probably not original. Sometimes you can tell where

repairs have been made, because of a change in the tapestry of the roof. The roof is the most important part of the barn, but also expensive to maintain. This is why some roofs are now sheet metal, visually a very poor substitute.

Look at the great doors on the side walls and visualize a fully loaded wagon with fresh-cut sheaves of grain squeezing into the door to be unloaded.

Now, walk into the barn and stand quietly at one end until your eyes adjust to the subdued light. Slowly, we think you will begin to feel the grandeur of the building, the simplicity of the space, the obvious functional purpose of the structure, for the protection of the harvest in the enclosure.

Now, start to enjoy some of the details. If it is a post and beam building, how are the posts set? If directly on the ground, it is a very old building; if on a timber sill, later; and probably still later if on a stone foundation. How are the diagonal braces attached to the uprights? If lapped, it is older, but if notched younger. With binoculars, you may be able to find a horizontal main timber lap joint. This will tell you how tall the best trees available at that time probably were.

If the barn has no aisle columns, then it may have been built with some form of cruck construction. The Middle Littleton barn has both post and beam aisles at each end and a very interesting cruck double tie beam construction for the rest of the barn. The Great Coxwell barn uses alternating post and beam and cruck trusses to create larger floor areas. The Leigh Court barn is the ultimate example of cruck construction.

Also with your binoculars, look for carpenters' marks at the joints and see if you can follow the progress of the original construction by the numbers etched on the beams.

Finally, but probably the most important of all, look for the stone thrashing floor between the great doors on opposite sides of the barn. This is where the harvest was turned into food, the ultimate purpose of the barn.

When you leave the barn, look to see if there is a Parish Church close by. If there is, see if you can pay it a visit. Recently, because of greater need for security, many of them are locked, but if the door is open, walk in and have a second quiet time. The church may be younger than the barn, but they will be close in age. However, the church close by the Ashleworth barn has evidence of Saxon masonry in the side wall, indicating a construction date of 1000 A.D. or earlier. Do not leave the church until you have left a donation in the wall box.

Now, go to a nearby pub and enjoy a ploughman's lunch. You have earned it.

Hint

If you want to take pictures inside the barn or church, the flash attachment to the camera will give you a good picture only for subjects 15 to 20 feet away. To get a picture of the whole interior, using ASA 100 or 200 film, stop the lens down to f8 and use an exposure time of 3-5 seconds. Use a tripod, or make sure the camera is held perfectly still by bracing it against a column or a wall.

A Partial Inventory of Medieval Barns

WHEN WE FIRST BECAME INTERESTED IN old barns, we wondered if there was a central source of information. We had seen a few barns that were under the protection of the National Trust, but realized there must be many more. Someone suggested we visit the offices of the Society for the Protection of Ancient Buildings (SPAB), located in London. So we found its address and, with a London map, found its street and started out. The building looked like it was right out of *David Copperfield*. The society office seemed to be located quite properly in a converted ancient dwelling. We walked into a dimly lit central hall where a woman behind a desk greeted us. When we explained our interest and said that we would like to talk to someone about it, we were asked, "Are you a member of the society?"

"No."

Next, "Do you have an appointment?"

No, we didn't have an appointment, and we would only be in London that day.

"Well, it is our policy to see non-member visitors only by appointment."

As we turned to leave, a voice came down the stairs from an upper room, suggesting that we wait a moment. Soon we were invited up the black oak staircase to a room that looked like the private library of a scholarly English gentleman. It was the office of Mrs. Dance, the director of the society. "I heard that American accent and became curious," she said. Mrs. Dance obviously was in command and knew her subject. The society had done little with barns because of its enormous need to help with other old buildings. However, she did get down from one of her wall library shelves a small, four by five-inch, forty-page booklet, prepared about 1930, titled *Notes on Ancient Barns*. This seemed to be the only centralized listing of ancient barns that existed at the time. The list was very useful to us and was our first guide. After that visit to SPAB we joined the society. The society has expanded greatly, moved to new quarters and, when possible, helped with barn restoration. We find their publications very informative and interesting.

To read about a medieval or Tithe Barn may be interesting, but the real thrill comes with an actual visit. The barns are listed alphabetically. If you know the name of a barn you wish to see, you can locate it easily. The list comes from a large number of sources, all of which are noted in the bibliography. For this inventory, all barns that were built after 1555, even though they may be called Tithe Barns, are not included. Please realize that this list is not complete. It is a selected index. So far as we know, there is no official list. As you travel about and ask questions, you will find other barns to add.

We have seen more than half of these barns, but it must be remembered that a barn is a living and dying object, and it may have changed considerably since our last visit.

NOTES

The abbreviations for the books that contain illustrations and information on some of the barns are as follows:

BG   *Blue Guide*
BRB   *Barns of Rural Britian*
ECFH *English Cottages and Farm Houses*
EHC   *English Historic Carpentry*
SS   *Silent Spaces*

NT   Indicates a National Trust property

Abbotsbury   *Dorset*, near Weymouth
          Benedictine Abbey barn built circa 1400
Originally 276 x 31 feet; old foundations still there, smaller now; outside stair tower leading to upper room; corner and gable end buttresses

Ablington   *Gloucestershire*, NE of Cirencester
          Double barn. Stone thrashing floor. Ill. in *BRB*, p. 15, 130.

Alciston   *East Sussex*, SE of Lewes
          Built in 1575 by monks of Battle Abbey. 200 feet long; L-shaped; flint stone walls; "One of Britain's biggest and finest medieval barns," *BRB*, ill. p. 146.

Alport   *Derbyshire*, SE of Buxton near Haddon Hall
                              Harthill Hall Farm
          Stone barn built in the mid-1200s. "Limestone glens" (*BG*); ill. in *ECFH*, p. 34.

Ashford   *Kent*
          Aisled barn built in the 1400s. *SS*, p. 102-103

Ashleworth   *Gloucestershire*
NT.   N of Gloucester on the Canal
          Stone barn built between 1481-1515. 125 x 25 feet; two projecting porch bays; queen posts; nearby parish church worth a visit because one wall contains Saxon masonry

Avebury   *Wiltshire*
          Thatched barn. Agriculture museum located in an ancient stone circle also worth a visit

Barkway   *Hertfordshire*, S of Royston
NT. Timber-framed and clad tithe barn

Belchamp St. Paul   *Essex*, W of Sudbury
          Portions of barn may be the oldest in Britain. Surviving structural portions suggest it dates back to perhaps pre-Conquest. Analyzed carefully by Cecil A. Hewett in *English Historic Carpentry.*

Bisham *Buckinghamshire*, one half-mile S of Marlow
Augustinian priory *(BG)*. A good conversion of a barn into a dwelling, partly because the original barn was not too large.

Bishops Cleve *Gloucestershire*, N of Cheltenham
Built in the 1200s. Truncated; now village hall.

Black Notley *Essex*, S of Braintree,
3 mi from **Cressing Temple** *(BG)*
Aisled barn. Weather-boarded; eight bays; good carpenters' marks (YII/YIII); corrugated metal roof.

Bolton Abbey *Yorkshire*, near Wharfedale
Big, aisled barn begun 1100s(?), rebuilt 1700s. Probably more recent outside stone walls. Augustinian priory founded c. 1120, moved to site 1151.

Bourton-on-the-Hill *Gloucestershire*,
Rt. 44 W of Moreton-in-Marsh
About 100 feet long; stage at one end; floor slopes with hill. Good barn, well-maintained, used for socials.

Ashleworth

NOTES

Boxley   *Kent*, near Pilgrims Way to Canterbury, near Maidstone

Large barn built circa 1300. Located on grounds of a remnant of Boxley Abbey.

Bradford-on-Avon   Wiltshire, Barton Farm

NT. Built in the 1300s. 168' long *(BG)* x 30' wide; fourteen bays; unaisled, long and low with two side entrances; stone tile roof. Built by Abbot of Shaftesbury; excellent example of small Saxon church close by.

Ill. in *SS*, p. 18, 19, 109.

Boxley

Bredon *Worcestershire*, 3 mi NE of Tewkesbury
NT. Excellent large barn built in 1344. 130 x 40 feet, approx. 44 m long; two porches, one with unusual stone cowling; has a small room with a fireplace on second floor over doorway; recently restored after fire in 1980. Documented in book by F.W.B. Charles; ill. in *SS*, p. 32.

Bretforton *Gloucestershire*, near Evesham
Built circa 1220. Ill. in *BRB*, p. 121. near the church

Broomfield *Kent*, off 299 E of Herne Bay
Parsonage Farm
187 x 32.5 feet; it took 20 tons of wheat straw to replace the thatch in 1935.

NOTES

Bradford-on-Avon

NOTES

Brook
Kent, E of Ashford Wye College Agricultural Museum
Main posts cambered inwards.

Buckland Abbey
Devon, S of Tavistock off Rt. 386
NT. Large, stone-walled barn founded by Cistercians 1278-1300. 180' long x 32' wide x 60' high; timber truss roof spanning from wall to wall; on base of door on east wall are slots for insertion of threshold board; thatch replaced by slate in 1772. Last monastery founded in Britain by Cistercians; also controlled by Plymouth City Council.

Buriton
Hampshire, N of Portsmouth off Rt. 3
Historic tithe barn and church.

Caldecote
Hertfordshire, SW of Peterborough off Rt. 1
Side-aisled barn with flat stone slabs running on the floor from the side wall to support the aisle columns. Ill. in *ECFH*, p. 23.

Carlisle
Cumbria, located on the edge of Cathedral precincts
Built circa 1470. Approx. 36 x 100 feet; masons' marks on stonework. Made into parish meeting room, restored. Augustinian priory founded in 1093.

Cerne Abbas
Dorset, N of Dorchester, Rt. 352
Benedictine built in mid-1300s. 130 feet long; nine bays remain; made of flintstone with ashlar trim. Interesting example of partial conversion: south end of barn made into dwelling in late 1700s ("Gothic"), north end still used for storage.

Charlton Kings
Gloucestershire, E outskirts of Cheltenham
Smaller size.

Chesham Bois
Buckinghamshire, just S of Chesham
Manor barn built in 1607. Tithe barn and other barns adjacent.

Cholsey
Berkshire, SE of Oxford off Rt. 329
Built in 12 or 1300s? Largest barn ever built? 303' long x 54' wide x 51' high; tile roof 30,770 sq. ft. of 230,000 tiles. Demolished in 1815. See page 43.

Coggeshall
Essex, W of Colchester
NT. 130 feet long; six bays; aisles, king posts, two porches, tiled roof; bricks made on-site. "Oldest surviving timber-framed barn in Europe, dating from c. 1140 and originally part of the Cistercian monastery of Coggeshall," (*NT*, 1997, p. 34). Abbey founded by King Stephen in 1140, Cistercian in 1148.

Seen in 1979: terrible shape, owner trying to get permission to dismantle. Completely restored in 1980s by Coggeshall Grange Barn Trust, Braintree District and Essex County Councils.

Copdock   *Suffolk,* just W of Ipswich

Built in the 1500s. Crow-stepped gables, ten bays.

Cotehele   *Cornwall,* St. Dominick, N Saltash,
on Tamar River

NT. Built from 1485-1499. Built after the Battle of Bosworth, 1485; includes dovecote.

Cressing Temple   *Essex,* near Braintree SE
on 1018 about 3 miles

Barley Barn, built pre-1130. Wheat Barn built in late 1200s. Two great barns, now owned by Essex County and very well-preserved and presented for public visits. Very good publications of scholarly studies of history and structure. Ill. in *SS,* p. 18.

Cerne Abbas

NOTES

Doulting *Somerset,* E of Shepton Mallet
Built circa 1275. One of four surviving barns of Glastonbury Abbey; Doulting provided stone for Wells cathedral *(BG).* Ills. in *SS,* p. 99; *ECFH,* p. 43.

East Riddlesden Hall *Yorkshire,* NE of Keighley
NT. "Timber-framed Great Barn" (*NT,* 1997). Part of a National Trust Great House property.

Edlesborough *Buckinghamshire,* SW of Dunstable
155 x 30 feet; brick and timber. Church Farm

Englishcombe *Somerset,* just S of Bath
Interesting symbol on west end of barn, which was in poor condition.

East Riddlesden

English Frankton *Shropshire,*
N of Shrewsbury off Rt. 528
Hollies Farm

A small barn, 25 x 60 feet; internal framing very interesting with floor braces to side posts; the infill of the outside walls was made with wide oak boards fitted into vertical slots, some still intact. Very interesting construction that may or may not be a tithe barn; to lighten roof load, it now has corrugated asbestos sheets.

Enstone *Oxfordshire,* SW of Chipping Norton off Rt. 34
Built in 1382. Good condition, 90 x 30 feet; built by Walter Winiforton, Abbot of Winchcombe.

Falmer *Sussex,* outside Brighton E on 27
Large, thatched barn; 14th C. court farm.

Fairstead *Essex,* N of Chelmsford
Aisled, medieval barn

English Frankton

NOTES

Farningham *Kent,* S of Dartford off Rt. 225
Roman/Medieval. Roman masonry in walls and floor; Britain's best color-tiled medieval roof.

Faversham *Kent,* on farm of the royal Cluniac Abbey
Interesting use of upturned, forked tree trunk. Abbey founded by King Stephen, who is buried there. "Teynham, first place cherries and apples were grown in Kent." *(BG)* Ill. in *SS,* p. 124.

Felstead *Essex,* W of Braintree, Rt. 1417
159 feet long; eleven bays; three porches, corrugated roof; said to be largest barn in county of Essex.

Fingest *Buckinghamshire,* W of High Wycombe off M40

Fine brick and flint.

Frindsbury *Kent,* just W across the river from Rochester
Built in the 1300s. 204 x 35 feet; thirteen bays; crown post roof; finest interior in Kent. Ill. in *SS,* p. 114, 115, CP22.

Frindsbury

Frocester   *Gloucestershire,* S of Gloucester off Rt. 38

Large barn built from 1284-1306. 183 feet; thirteen bays; two wagon porches on same side; good interior roof construction; limestone, stone slate roof; part of a large farm complex. Built by John De Gamages, Abbot of Gloucester. (See Charles, *Journal of Society of Architectural Historians,* and Horn, 1963.)

Garstang   *Lancashire,* N of Preston off A6

Conversion to restaurant.

Glastonbury   *Somerset*

Built circa 1375. Good religious details in stonework at end of building; barn preserved and now a farm museum. Ills. in *SS*, p. 16, 17; *ECFH*, p. 42.

Godmersham   *Kent,* SW of Canterbury on 28 at Court Lodge

N O T E S

Glastonbury

NOTES

Grasmere Lake District, *Cumbria,* across the street from the church
Vicar called this a tithe barn; have not seen it, not listed in any other source.

Great Coxwell *Berkshire,* 2 mi SW of Faringdon
NT. Built in the 1200s. 152' long x 40' wide x 48' tall; stone tiled roof. Belonged to Cistercian Abbey of Beaulieu. Ill. in *SS*, p. 12, 14, 15. (See Horn & Born, 1965.)

Great Ponton *Lincolnshire,* S of Grantham on A1
95 x 24 feet; oak beams with good carpenters' marks; good condition, full of grain drying machinery.

Haddenham *Buckinghamshire,* SW of Aylesbury, near church and manor farmhouse
Large barn built in the 1400s. Six bays; aisles, tie beams on braces, diagonal queen posts.

Hales *Norfolk,* near Beccles
Built in 1480. Probably not a tithe barn.180 x 28 feet; brickwork and timber roof; living quarters built at one end; Dutch influence; interesting enough to deserve a visit. "Already by the Middle Ages, the major part was used as storage, with a dwelling and a partial intermediate floor at one end. Here is a medieval conversion which inserted small rooms in one end and left most of the big hall free for storage and agricultural use." (*BRB*)

Harmondsworth *Greater London,* a few miles W of Heathrow Airport
Good barn built 1426-27. 191 feet long; twelve bays; vertical tarred wood plank cladding; possibly built for William of Wykeham. Close to parish church; used by a truck farmer; one end burned and restored. Ill. in *SS*, p. 19.

Hartpury *Gloucestershire,* N of Gloucester on A417
Good medieval stonework; recent restoration.

Haseley *Oxfordshire,* SW of Kenilworth on A41
Aisled tithe barn built circa 1400. Seven bays, originally fourteen; arched wind braces.

Hawkshead *Cumbria* Field Head Farm
Good example of small cruck barn; well-maintained.

Heightley *Shropshire,* near Chirbury
Ten bays; brick; cusped wind braces.

Henley *Suffolk,* near Claydon, N of Ipswich
Built in the 1400s. Post and trusses building.

Herstmonceux *Sussex,* E of Hastings on B271
Rare 15th-century brickwork; town famous for trugs.

Highleadon   *Gloucester,* near Ashleworth, NW of
Gloucester off B4215
Nearly 200 feet long; currently used by local dairy.

High Roding   *Essex,* W of Braintree on Rt. 184
Reportedly built in 1488. Seven bays; king post roof; very interesting brick infill with different patterns for each space between the upright exterior timbers.

Hill Deveril   Devizes, *Wiltshire*
Cromwell's soldiers slept here and used it to stable their horses. Used for wedding receptions and barn dances.

Hinton St. Mary   *Dorset,* SW of Shaftesbury,
B3092, by church
Large barn built in the 1400s. Converted to theatre.

Hawkshead, Field Head farm

NOTES

Kewstoke   *Avon,* N edge of Weston-Super-Mare
Woodspring Priory, built circa 1300. Well-maintained barn full of straw at the time of our visit. Controlled by Landmark Trust.

Kington St. Michael   *Wiltshire,* N of Chippenham
off A429
Farm was originally St. Mary's Priory. Small, about 60 x 24 feet; building well-restored and in good condition.

Lacock   *Wiltshire,* on A350 S of Chippenham
NT. Built in the 1300. In town; Abbey founded 1232. Interesting feature: end is not square in order to accommodate road.

Lawkland   *Yorkshire,* Lawkland Hall, W of Settle off A65
Doors and roof in need of repair; east end converted for living quarters; two feet deep in winter manure when seen in 1979.

Lacock

Layer Marney   *Essex,* SW of Colchester off B1022

Large barn built in 1525. Mostly timber, brick lower walls.

Leigh Court   *Worcestershire,* 5 mi W of Worcester

Built in the early 1300s. 34 x 140 feet; ten bays; brick, clapboard, tile roof; cruck construction, largest in the country. Crucks are paired timbers each about 36' long (*BRB*). Originally belonged to the Benedictine Abbey of Pershore. Well worth a visit; owned and preserved by British Heritage. Ill. in *SS*, p. 108.

Leiston Abbey   *Suffolk,* N of Ipswich on B1119

Built circa 1400. Thatched roof of Norfolk reed; brick, stone, chalk and flint; no aisles; tie beam and collar roof with no struts or vertical braces or posts. Now a concert and assembly hall.

Lenham   *Kent,* SE of Maidstone, by the church

Thatched masterpiece built in the 1300s. 160 feet long; seven bays; two doors each side. Ill. in *SS*, p. 100, 101, 123.

Linton   *Yorkshire,* N of Keighley on B6265

Has ventilation openings very much like windows on a Saxon church with a single, arched cut stone spanning the opening.

Lenham

NOTES

Littlebourne *Kent*, E of Canterbury
Perhaps built just after 1300 (see **Frindsbury**). 172 feet long, wider than **Frindsbury**; seven full bays; thatched roof. Original single entry changed to two. One of the barns of St. Augustine's Abbey, Canterbury.

Little Wymondley *Hertfordshire*, just W of Stevenage
Built in the 1200s.

Macaroni Farm *Gloucestershire*, near Northleach, E of Cheltenham
Good group with typical local overhanging lip on double porches (*BRB*).

Maiden Newton *Dorset*, NW of Dorchester
Thatched roof; church and barn located next to each other.

Manuden *Essex*, NW of Bishop's Stortford
Pink plaster on brick and flint base.

Methley *West Yorkshire*, 7 mi SE of Leeds on B6135

Middle Littleton *Worcestershire*, S of Stratford-on-Avon on B4085
NT. Built in the 1200s. 142 x 38 feet; double tie beams; blue lias stone. Fine example restored about 1975.

North Benfleet *Essex*, N of Basildon
Roof built in 1610. Tithe barn with tiled roof.

Nupend *Hereford and Worcestershire*, W of Stroud near the M5
Great tithe barn, used as antiques and exhibition gallery.

Odstock *Wiltshire*, just S of Salisbury
Odstock Manor Farm
Aisled barn built of flint rubble; timbering remarkably heavy.

Old Basing *Hampshire*, near Basingstoke Grange Farm
Built in the early 1500s. Fine brickwork, excellent timber roof interior and buttresses; maintained by the community.

Oxford *Oxfordshire*
Fine exterior, original roof with king posts. Built in 1402. Warden's Barn, New College, now part of college accommodations.

Paston *Norfolk*, NE of Norwich, near the shore
Stone on North Wall shows date 1581. 150 x 26 feet; full of potatoes and straw when we saw it.

Patcham *East Sussex*, near Brighton
Possibly the longest barn in Britain, 250 feet; flint walls.

Penistone   *Yorkshire,* on A628
Gunthwaite Hall

Built circa 1568-1580. 163 x 44 feet; eleven bays; heavy, king post roof truss. Ill. in *SS*, p. 112, 113.

Pilton   *Somerset,* E of Glastonbury

Said to date from Richard II. 108 x 44 feet; religious carvings in the walls; one of the Glastonbury barns. Fire in 1963 destroyed the ten timber roof trusses; now a ruin with only end walls standing. Ill. in *SS*, p. 21; *ECFH*, p. 43.

Pinner   *Greater London,* Headstone Lane, near station
Headstone Manor

Located in a park off Headstone Road; used for concerts and meetings, as tearoom and for display of local crafts. Visited 9/3/97, took pictures; worth a visit if you are close by.

Pirton   *Hereford,* W of Letchworth

Cruck frame.

NOTES

Paston

NOTES

Prestbury   *Cheshire*, N of Macclesfield
Tytherington Old Hall Farm
Good shape and repair. Hamlet of Tytherington in old times was called "Tithe Town."

Preston Plucknett   *Somerset*, W area of Yeovil
Built circa 1400. South exterior of barn carefully preserved; north side and interior converted to a storage area and work room for a construction company; interesting conversion.

Rivington   *Lancashire*, S of Chorley near M61
Cruck barn. Now used as a recreation center.

Rogate   *Hampshire*, E of Petersfield
Typical timber cladding; characteristic, huge thatched porches *(BRB)*.

Rotherham   *South Yorkshire*, NE of Sheffield
Whiston Hall Barn
Tree ring dating suggests construction 1196-1204.

Ruislip   *Greater London*
Built before 1324. Originally owned by King's College, Cambridge; currently being used for storage. Second barn close by converted into a library. Visited 9/3/97; not open to visitors; bought a good folder on the barn at the library and had a pleasant lunch at the tea room in adjacent building.

Shipton-under-Wychwood   *Oxfordshire*, N of Burford on Rt. 361
Built in the 1400s. At old prebendal house; barn now redundant; threat of demolition.

Siddington   *Gloucestershire*, outskirts S of Cirencester
Typical Cotswold barn, built circa 1300. Five bays; stone-walled; recent applications to demolish withdrawn after protests. Built when the Cotswolds dominated Europe's wool industry (*EHC*, p. 87-88).

South Benfleet   *Essex*, outskirts of Basildon
Tithe barn situated on the main road.

Snape   *Suffolk*, W of Aldeburgh on A1094
Probably oldest in Suffolk. Part of Snape Abbey Foundation *(BRB)*.

Standon   *Hertfordshire*, N of Hertford on A120
Tree ring dating suggests construction c. 1240. One of Standonbury Barns.

Stanton   *Gloucestershire*, SW of Broadway, near church
Typical tithe barn built in the 1300s. Now used as a meeting place on property of Earl of Wemyes.

Stanway *Gloucestershire*, SW of Broadway
Field barn. Isolated site near a cottage. Converted by architect Jeremy Benson, Vice Chairman of SPAB; new inside and out, new timbers, large chimneys, huge interior room.

Stoke-sub-Hamdon Priory *Somerset*, just W of Yeovil
NT. Begun in the 1300s Good thatched stone group; built for Chantry Chapel of St. Nicholas. Near famous limestone quarries of Ham Hill. *(BG)*

Stonham Parva *Suffolk*, N of Ipswich

Stowupland *Suffolk*, just NE of Stowmarket
Three threshing floors; fine central position in village.

Sturry *Kent,* just N of Canterbury on A28
Brick barn built in the 1500s. Two side doors; well-cared for; part of grounds of school; used for school events.

Sydling St. Nicholas *Dorset*, N of Dorchester off A37
In fair condition; second door cut crudely in the side through the stone wall. Said to have the initials of Lady Ursula Walsingham, 1490, but we could not find them. Located next to church graveyard.

Temple Cressing See **Cressing Temple**
Names are used interchangeably in English sources.

Sydling, St. Nicholas

NOTES

Thame   *Oxfordshire,* E of Oxford, Church Road
Built in the 1500s. Very large, 3-story; half-timbered; fine exterior; now used for storing books.

Thorley   *Hertfordshire,* just S of Bishop's Stortford
Restored in 1995; now church hall of St. James the Great.

Tisbury   *Wiltshire,* E of Salisbury
Place Farm
189 x 32 feet; thatched roof; original timbers. Once a grange of the Abbesses of Shaftesbury.

Titchfield Abbey   *Hampshire,* just W of Fareham
Big barn built before 1400. 150 x 37 feet; wall and roof patterns; some rebuilding. "One of finest medieval barns in country." (*BRB*)

Torquay   *Devon,* Torre Abbey
Built circa 1300. Lancet windows.

Tredrea   Perranaworthal, *Cornwall,* 4.5 mi SW of Truro
"One of Britain's largest barns." (*BRB*)

Tisbury

Upminster *Greater London,* Hall Lane, within 3/4 mi of Metropolitan Underground Station

Hall Barn probably built in the mid-1400s. Aisled with crown posts, four bays on either side of central midstrey; thatched roof, weather-boarded; scarf joints are edge-halved and bridle-butted with four face pegs and two edge pegs. New College Oxford was the big, local landowner; now a folk, agricultural and local history museum. Scheduled Ancient Monument; compare with **Ruislip**, **Pinner** and **Hammondsworth** for greater London area.

Upper Heyford *Oxfordshire,* near the Oxford Canal, S of Banbury

Built for William of Wykeham in the 1400s. Property of Winchester Cathedral.

Wanborough *Surry,* just W of Guildford

Restored 1997.

Waxham *Norfolk,* N of Great Yarmouth on the Shore

180 x 30 feet; brick wall patterning; good timber work for roof, which was probably thatched, though roof at one end in poor shape.

NOTES

Waxham

NOTES

Wellingborough *Hereford*
Converted by local authority *(BRB)*.

Wells *Somerset*, near the Cathedral
Bishop's Barn built circa 1400. Now used for public meetings.

Wendens Ambo *Essex*, just W of Saffron Walden
Mutlow Farm
Built in the 1400s. 32 x 150 feet; three gabled porches; black, clapboard sides; low-pitched, thatched roof; sill beams on brick foundations. A good barn to visit. Ill. in *ECFH*, p. 25.

Westdean *East Sussex*, near Litlington
Three large tithe barns converted together by architect Wycliffe Sturchbury. "Fourth bigger barn is drastic conversion." (*BRB*)

West Dean *Wiltshire*, E of Salisbury
Thirteen bays; brick buttressed.

Westenhanger *Kent*, W of Hythe, near M20, at Newingreen
Built mostly in the 1400s. Large L-shaped plan; hammer-beam roof.

West Pennard

West Malling   *Kent,* W of Maidstone, near M20
    Built in the 1400s. Now chapel for an enclosed, contemplative order (Benedictine). Converted by architect Robert Maguire.

West Meon   *Hampshire,* SW of Winchester on A32
    Small barn. Five bays; rescued by owner-farmer in 1980.

West Pennard   *Somerset,* just E of Glastonbury
NT. "Court barn" built in the 1400s. Five bays; combined with a dovecote. One of the Glastonbury Barns. Repaired and given by SPAB in 1938.

Westwood Manor   *Wiltshire,* SW of Bradford-on-Avon,
NT. Built in the 1400s.   E of church

Widdington   *Essex,* S of Saffron Walden
    110 x 36 feet; large porches; central roof ridge beam; tiled roof; weather-boarded walls; ogee-shaped support braces for the crown post. On our first visit in 1979, this barn was under repair with the roof off and interior full of scaffolding; long restoration; now open to visitors.

Winchcombe   *Gloucestershire,* NE of Cheltenham,
Rt. 46, at back of main street

Winterslow   *Wiltshire,* NE of Salisbury
    Roche Old Court, built in the 1400s. Oak beams.

Witham Parva   *Essex*
Powers Hall Farm
    Built in the early 1400s(?). 36 x 110 feet; seven bays; two porches, aisles, wind braces; roof originally thatched; good condition.

Woodspring Priory   *Avon*
    See **Kewstoke**

Wyke   *Dorset,* NE of Shaftesbury
    Two barns in continuous range, about 230 feet long; buttressed walls; collar beams and curved wind braces in fine roofs.

NOTES   *Counties of England*

Avon 33
Bedfordshire 30
Berkshire 35
Buckinghamshire 29
Cambrdigeshire 24
Cheshire 13
Cleveland 5
Cornwall and Isles
   of Scilly 41
Cumbria 2
Derbyshire 14
Devon 42
Dorset 43
Durham 3
East Sussex 46
Essex 32
Gloucestershire 27
Greater London 36
Greater Manchester 9
Hampshire 38
Hereford and
   Worcestershire 21
Hertfordshire 31
Humberside 12
Isle of Wight 44
Kent 40
Lancashire 6
Leicestershire 19
Lincolnshire 16
Merseyside 8

Norfolk 25
Northamptonshire 23
Northumberland 1
North Yorkshire 7
Nottinghamshire 15
Oxfordshire 28
Salop 17
Somerset 37
South Yorkshire 11
Staffordshire 18
Suffolk 26
Surrey 39
Tyne and Wear 4
West Midlands 20
West Yorkshire 10
Warwickshire 22
West Sussex 45
Wiltshire 34
Yorkshire 7, 10, 11

Tithe Barns Listed by English Counties

33 AVON
Kewstoke

35 BERKSHIRE
Cholsey
Great Coxwell

29 BUCKINGHAMSHIRE
Bisham
Chesham Bois
Edlesborough
Fingest
Haddenham

13 CHESHIRE
Prestbury

41 CORNWALL
Cotehele
Tredrea

2 CUMBRIA
Carlisle
Grasmere
Hawkshead

14 DERBYSHIRE
Alport

42 DEVON
Buckland Abbey
Torquay

43 DORSET
Abbotsbury
Cerne Abbas
Hinton St. Mary
Maiden Newton
Sydling St. Nicholas
Wyke

46 EAST SUSSEX
Alciston
Falmer
Herstmonceux
Patcham
Westdean

32 ESSEX
Belchamp St. Paul
Black Notley
Coggeshall
Cressing Temple
Fairstead
Felstead
High Roding
Layer Marney
Manuden
North Benfleet
South Benfleet
Wendens Ambo
Widdington
Witham Parva

27 GLOUCESTERSHIRE
Ablington
Ashleworth
Bishop's Cleve
Bourton-on-the-Hill
Bretforton
Charlton Kings
Frocester
Hartpury
Highleadon
Macaroni Farm
Siddington
Stanton
Stanway
Winchcombe

36 GREATER LONDON
Harmondsworth
Pinner
Ruislip
Upminster

38 HAMPSHIRE
Buriton
Old Basing
Rogate
Titchfield Abbey
West Meon

21 HEREFORD and
WORCESTERSHIRE
Bredon
Leigh Court
Middle Littleton
Nupend
Pirton
Wellingborough

31 HERTFORDSHIRE
Barkway
Caldecote
Little Wymondley
Standon
Thorley

40 KENT
Ashford
Boxley
Broomfield
Brook
Farningham
Faversham
Frindsbury
Godmersham
Lenham
Littlebourne
Sturry
Westenhanger
West Malling

6 LANCASHIRE
Garstang
Rivington

16 LINCOLNSHIRE
Great Ponton

25 NORFOLK
Hales
Paston
Waxham

28 OXFORDSHIRE
Enstone
Haseley
Oxford
Shipton-under-
Wychwood
Thame
Upper Heyford

17 SHROPSHIRE (Salop)
English Frankton
Heightley

37 SOMERSET
Doulting
Englishcombe
Glastonbury
Kewstoke
Pilton
Preston Plucknet
Stoke-sub-Hamdon
Wells
West Pennard

26 SUFFOLK
Copdock
Henley near Claydon
Leiston Abbey
Snape
Stonham Parva
Stowupland

39 SURREY
Wanborough

34 WILTSHIRE
Avebury
Bradford-on-Avon
Hill Deveril
Kington St. Michael
Lacock
Odstock
Tisbury
West Dean
Westwood Manor
Winterslow

7, 10, 11 YORKSHIRE
Bolton Abbey
East Riddlesden
Lawkland
Linton
Methley
Penistone
Rotherham

Warning

It is possible that a visit to any one or more of the following very choice barns may cause you to become a barnaholic!

Bredon
Buckland Abbey
Coggeshall
Cressing Temple (two barns)
Frocester
Great Coxwell
Leigh Court
Middle Littleton

1. The Tithe Barn located at Paul's Hall, Belchamp, Saint Paul, Essex, is documented in Cecil A. Hewett's *English Historic Carpentry*.

2. Weller, H., 1986. *Grangia Et Orreum*, Biddeston Booklets. From page 34 of *Cressing Temple*, prepared by Essex County Council.

3. Taken from pages 85-92 of article by Oliver Rackham, Corpus Christi College, Cambridge. In *Cressing Temple*, prepared by Essex County Council.

4. *Ibid.* page 87.

5. This is a calculated guess. Our local lumber dealer who specializes in hardwoods told me that 100 board feet of green oak would weigh 580 pounds. At 5.8 pounds per square board foot a cubic foot would weigh 69.6 pounds. Another source, *Wood* (Taunton Press) has a chart that gives the specific gravity of various oak species and they range from .60 to .80 for green wood. Taking an average of the above would give .70. A cubic foot of water weighs 62 pounds so a cubic foot of green oak with a gravity of .70 would weigh 43.2 pounds.

6. From technical preface section, page VIII of F.W.B. Charles' book *The Great Barn of Bredon*.

7. If you can manage to get into an area where you can inspect the timber joints of an American house, church, or barn built before 1800, you may find these same carpenters' marks, revealing a building tradition that is at least six hundred years old.

8. From Horn and Born's book on Great Coxwell, page XIII.

9. From Cecil A. Hewett, *English Historic Carpentry*, page 188.

10. Hewett notes from Dr. J.H. Harvey, *The Medieval Architect (1972)* as follows..."the greatest single work of art of the whole of the European Middle Ages. No such comparable achievement in the fields of mechanics and aesthetics remains elsewhere, nor is there any evidence for such a feat having ever existed."

11. Comment paraphrased from page 216-217 of *London, As Seen and Described by Famous Writers*, edited by Esther Singleton. New York, Dodd Mead and Company, 1902.

12. Because this book does not provide all the wonderful supporting information that is in Mr. Hewett's book, this drawing has been enhanced considerably.

13. The dimensions of each roof are approximately 42 by 150 feet, not counting the roofs for side porches.

14. Horn and Born's book on the Great Coxwell Barn presents this study in great detail with many drawings on pages 26-31.

15. From article on "The Great Tithe Barn of Cholsey" by Walter Horn.

BIBLIOGRAPHY

Alcock, N.W. *A Catalogue of Cruck Buildings.* London and Chicester: Phillimore & Co., Ltd., 1973.

Andrews, D.D. Ed. *Cressing Temple, A Templar and Hospitaller Manor in Essex.* Chelmsford, England: Essex County Council, 1993.

Armstrong, J.R. *Traditional Buildings—Accessible to the Public.* Wakefield, West Yorkshire: EP Publishing, Ltd., 1979.

Beacham, M.J.A. *Tithe Barns, Midlands.* Studley, Warwickshire: KAF Brewin Books, 1987.

———. *Tithe Barns, West Country.* Studley, Warwickshire: KAF Brewin Books, 1987.

The Bible. The New English Edition, Oxford, Oxford University Press, 1970.

Charles, F.W.B. *The Great Barn of Bredon, Its Fire and Reconstruction.* Park End Place, Oxford, Oxbow Books: 1997.

Charles, F.W.B. and Walter Horn. "The cruck-built barn of Frocester Court Farm, Gloucestershire, England." *Journal of the Society of Architectural Historians,* October 1983; 42(3).

Clark, Henry William, Rev. *A History of Tithes.* London: Swan, Sonnenschein & Co., 1891.

Cook, Olive. *English Cottages and Farmhouses.* New York, Thames and Hudson, 1982

Cordingley, R.A. "British historical roof-types and their members: a classification." Reprint from the *Transactions of the Ancient Monument Society,* New Series, Vol. 9, 1961.

County Planner, County Hall, Chelmsford, Essex. *Historic Barns, the Essex Countryside: a Planning Appraisal.*

Easterby, William. *History of the Law of Tithes in England.* Cambridge University Press, 1888. NOTE: We found Easterby to be a good source of information, and much of what we have written came from this book.

Endersby, Greenwood, and Larkin. *Barn: the Art of a Working Building.* New York: Houghton Mifflin, 1992.

Harris, Richard. *Discovering Timber-Framed Buildings.* Aylesbury: Shire Publications, Ltd., 1978.

Hewett, Cecil A. "Aisled timber halls and related buildings, chiefly in Essex." Reprint from the *Transactions of the Ancient Monument Society,* New Series, Vol. 21, 1976.

———. *English Historic Carpentry.* London and Chichester: Phillimore & Co., Ltd., 1980.

———. "The barns at Cressing Temple, Essex." *Journal of the Society of Architectural Historians,* March 1967; 26(1).

Horn, Walter. "The great tithe barn of Cholsey." *Journal of the Society of Architectural Historians,* March 1963; 22(1).

Horn, Walter and Ernest Born. *A Victim of Fire: the 15th Century Manor Barn of Nettlestead Place, Kent.* Aachen: Aachener Kunstblatter, 1969.

———. *The Barns of the Abbey of Beaulieu at its Granges of Great Coxwell and Beaulieu St. Leonards.* Berkeley: University of California Press, 1965.

Horn, Walter and F.W.B. Charles. "The cruck-built barn of Middle Littleton in Worcestershire, England." *Journal of the Society of Architectural Historians,* December 1966; 25(4).

Horwath, David. *1066: The Year of the Conquest.* New York: Penguin Books, 1981.

Hughes, Graham. *Barns of Rural Britain.* London: The Herbert Press, 1985.

Hunter, John. "Historic landscape of Cressing Temple and its environs." In *Cressing Temple,* p. 25.

Kirk, Malcolm. *Silent Spaces: The Last of the Great Aisled Barns.* Boston: Bulfinch Press Books, Little Brown & Co, 1994.

Muirhead, L. Russell, ed. *Blue Guides; England.* London, Benn, 1965 and later editions.

The National Trust. *Handbook for Members and Visitors.* London: The National Trust, 1996.

Rackham, Oliver. "Woodland management and timber economy as evidenced by the buildings at Temple Cressing." In *Cressing Temple,* p. 85.

Schaefer, Vincent J. *Dutch Barns of New York.* Fleischmanns, NY: Purple Mountain Press, 1994.

Seldon, John. *The History of Tythes.* Printed in London, 1618.
NOTE: It is hard to describe what a thrill it was to find this book in the Rare Books section of the Boston Public Library. I was allowed to hold it in my hand and try to read it. Because the English language has changed so much in nearly four centuries, and we are not trained in this skill, it was very difficult. However, it is interesting to see how many references Easterby has to the work of Seldon. A note attached to the Seldon book said that at the time of printing, the subject of tithing was highly controversial, and by royal order the books were collected and burned. Fortunately, this copy got to Boston. We understand there is another copy at the Huntington Library in California.

Singleton, Esther, ed. *London, As Seen and Described by Famous Writers*, New York, Dodd Mead, 1902.

SPAB. *The Barns Book.* London: The Society for the Protection of Ancient Buildings, 1982.

Students at the School of Architecture, Canterbury College of Art, Studies by. *Traditional Kent Buildings.* Kent County Council, 1980.

Thompson, Thomas. *Origins and Effects of Tithes.* Hull, 1795.

Walker, Aidan., Gen. Ed. *The Encyclopedia of Wood.* London: Quarto Publishing, 1989.

Wood: the Best of Fine Woodworking. Newtown, CT: The Taunton Press, 1995.

If you are not already a member of the National Trust (NT) in England, we recommend that you join at your first visit to one of its properties. The trust is a charitable organization, founded in 1895, that now protects and opens to the public more than two hundred historic houses, 160 gardens, and twenty-five industrial monuments. Among these properties are seven Tithe Barns. The National Trust barns are indicated by the letters NT in the listing of Tithe Barns in the back of this book.

The English Heritage organization is another important force for the preservation of historic structures, and likewise deserves our support. Also, the Landmark Trust has saved many interesting ancient buildings and converted them into holiday residences. They can provide you with a listing of vacation sites. And, finally, the Society for the Protection of Ancient Buildings (SPAB), at 37 Spital Square, London, is a fine institution dedicated to preservation.

A Possibly Apocryphal Story

Frank Lloyd Wright (1869-1952), the noted American architect, is remembered for his design of the Imperial Hotel in Tokyo, which withstood the great earthquake that wiped out the city's downtown, and of the Guggenheim Art Museum in New York City, famous for its continuous, ascending spiral ramp for viewing paintings. Wright was asked in 1930 to come to London to give a series of lectures. (This part we know is true.) Upon his arrival by ship at Southhampton, the visiting committee asked him what special, architecturally significant buildings of the many that are located in England he would like to see. His immediate reply was, "The Tithe Barn at Great Coxwell, England's greatest architectural achievement."

Wright was known to have been a self-centered individual, one who might have considered himself as the greatest living architect in the world, and he might not have wanted to compliment any English architect by visiting a contemporary building.